ADOLESCENCE

Positive approaches for working with young people

Ann Wheal

TU

RHP

ADOLESCENCE: Positive approaches for working with young people

Russell House Publishing Limited

First published in 1998, and reprinted in 1999, by:
Russell House Publishing Limited
4 St. George's House
The Business Park
Uplyme Road
Lyme Regis
Dorset DT7 3LS

© Ann Wheal

British Library Cataloguing-in-Publication Data:
A catalogue record for this manual is available from the British Library.

ISBN: 1-898924-19-8

Design and layout by: Jeremy Spencer, London

Printed by Cromwell Press, Trowbridge

Contents

Acknowledgements

My grateful thanks must go to:

All the professionals and young people who helped so willingly with their comments and suggestions.

To my dear friends Pat Proctor and Brenda Hughes for their help.

To Prim Upton, the inspiration for this book – the only lecturer who gave me any practical suggestions for achieving success with young people.

To my husband Peter for his patience, tolerance and love.

Publisher's note

Current differences between the law in England, Scotland and Northern Ireland have been highlighted within the text. Knowing which are the applicable Acts will enable you to check on up-to-date amendments or guidance.

DIGNITY

"We learn, when we respect the dignity of the people, that they cannot be denied the elementary right to participate fully in the solutions to their own problems. Self-respect arises only out of people who play an active role in solving their own crises and who are not helpless, passive puppet-like recipients of private or public services. To give people help, while denying them a significant part of the action, contributes nothing to the development of the individual. In the deepest sense, it is not giving but taking their dignity. Denial of opportunity for participation is the denial of human dignity and democracy. It will not work."

Quote from *Rules for Radicals* by Saul D. Alinsky, 1971, Vintage Books, A division of Random House, New York, 1972.

Foreword

During the last 25 years I have been a teacher in inner-city multi-racial schools and colleges; a youth worker; a volunteer in a secure unit; an academic researcher meeting young people from many different races, cultures, classes and backgrounds including young offenders. I have also run groups both for, and with, young people and helped one group to establish their own youth club.

It is from this broad perspective of working with adolescents that this book has been written.

The book is intended for anyone new to front line youth work, social work, foster care, residential care and teaching. It is also intended for experienced practitioners who sometimes find that certain strategies no longer work, either because they have changed or perhaps because young people today have different expectations and beliefs. It will also be useful to researchers as a first source of reference to give them background information on positive strategies.

The aim of this book is to help anyone working with adolescents to understand young people better, and to achieve success, both for themselves but especially for the young person. It is certainly hoped that someone reading the book from end to end will profit from doing so. But theory, research, practical suggestions plus comments from young people are combined in such a way that the reader can find all these things in one place when they dip into whichever part of the book is appropriate to their needs at any one time.

Too often simple reminders are all that is required to prevent a small incident becoming a major disaster. It is hoped that *Adolescence* will help meet this need.

Chapter 1

Introduction

Working with young people can be a thankless task. It can also be a very rewarding way of life. This book is for carers, social workers, teachers, youth workers, students and even parents. What it aims to do is to assist anyone working with young people to:

- create an environment where each young person is treated as an individual with respect and dignity
- help young people to achieve their potential in all the facets of their life
- give them opportunities to learn new skills and discover new experiences
- help them to learn to understand and tolerate other people's points of view and respect their feelings
- prepare them as far as possible for a happy and self-fulfilling adulthood.

The book has been written in consultation with young people and a wide variety of professionals including youth workers, teachers, care workers, foster carers, policy makers and police. It draws on a variety of resources – books, training material, research reports, academic papers and journals as well as on the author's own experience of over 20 years working with, and advocating for, young people in a variety of circumstances. All the scenarios and quotations are true and it is hoped that this personalising will make the information more pertinent.

Much of the material in the book is designed to assist adults but equally it can be used to assist young people to achieve successfully their transition to adulthood. This is particularly true of the chapter on communication.

Conversely, many of the suggestions in the book are equally relevant to achieving success with colleagues, superiors and subordinates.

Working with adolescents cannot and never will be just a job. It must be a vocation. However, even the most dedicated adult will become disillusioned if the right environment is not created or the people concerned are not trained to achieve these goals.

A recent leaflet on drug abuse listed some features that might help to identify a drug user, such as staying in bed late, being uncommunicative, morose, looking pale and unkempt or repeatedly playing very loud music. Anyone who has worked with young people will know that this description could refer to almost anyone at some time during their teenage life. There is a great danger that a young person may be given the wrong label which sticks. Those working with that young person make decisions around that label rather than looking at the individual who may experiment, stretch boundaries and generally try to discover their own identity as major physical and emotional changes take place.

The media puts enormous pressure on young people to wear particular clothes, use make-up, listen to this music, watch certain videos and generally behave in a manner beyond their years. This means that they may miss out on the latter part of their childhood and are expected to conform to certain media induced behaviour patterns. It is little wonder then that teenage behaviour often causes conflict. When they are with their friends and having fun – often what is quite innocent fun – this is misunderstood and labelled disruptive.

For the purpose of this book adolescence means young people aged 12-16 years. The age band is only a guideline as much of the information will be relevant to the under 12s and over 16s. It all depends upon the young person. Everyone is different. What is important is that each is treated as an individual. What works for A one day may not work the next day or week, or will not work at all for B.

The book does not set out to give all the answers, more to enhance the awareness and understanding of teenage years and to give some suggestions for strategies which should assist in achieving success with, and for, young people. It is also suitable for trainers as many of the approaches mentioned may be expanded for use as part of general staff training.

FICE (Fédération Internationale des Communicatives Éducatives) has developed the following summarised code of ethics for those working with young people.

It is the professional responsibility of everyone to:

- **value and respect a young person** as an individual in their own right, in their role as a member of their family and in their role as a member of the community in which he or she lives

- **respect the relationship of the young person to their parents, their siblings** and other members of their family, taking account of their natural ties and interdependent rights and responsibilities

- **enable the normal growth and development** of each individual young person to achieve his or her potential in all aspects of functioning

- **help each young person** for whom he or she bears responsibility by preventing problems where possible, by offering protection where necessary, or by providing care and rehabilitation to counteract or resolve problems faced

- **use information appropriately**, respecting the privacy of young people, maintaining confidentiality where necessary and avoiding the misuse of personal information

- **oppose at all times any form of discrimination**, oppression or exploitation of young people and preserve their rights

- **maintain personal and professional integrity**, develop skills and knowledge in order to work with competence, work co-operatively with colleagues, monitor the quality of services, and contribute to the development of the service and of policy and thinking in the field.

The ethos and principles that underpin this book are based around these seven clauses.

Chapter 2

Understanding adolescents

"The two most difficult times of life are when you are a teenager and when you have or have to care for a teenager" – the mother of 3 adolescents quoted in *Parenting Teens, A Road Map through the Ages and Stages of Adolescence*, Bruce Narramore and Vern C. Lewis.

Social workers, youth workers, youth justice, the probation service and the teaching profession have all come under fire in recent years from ill-informed critics including politicians and the media. Procedures, forms and assessments have all been allowed to get in the way of professionals achieving success with young people.

There is, of course, no right answer to achieving success. Every young person is different and must be treated differently.

Whilst researching this book professionals were asked what they felt was important when working with adolescents. The following statements were made which have been listed in no particular order:

- establish clear expectations and limits
- discipline fairly
- deal with negative behaviour in a positive way
- reward good behaviour
- promote and encourage a relationship with birth family if appropriate whilst the young person is being looked after
- encourage a young person's cultural and religious heritage and behave in a way which does not discriminate
- ensure that the young person's educational needs are met
- promote a young person's self-esteem and positive self-image
- respect the young person and their birth family

- work with all concerned, including young people themselves, to help them achieve their potential
- help the young person to learn to live independently
- help the young person to speak up, to be heard and to be listened to
- listen, understand and relate to each young person
- be available when needed
- encourage independent thinking
- be knowledgeable about sexuality
- beware of over or under stimulation
- allow them their own space and privacy
- learn to handle hypersensitivity
- provide stability and structure
- share your own adolescent experiences
- know their friends
- set realistic limits
- encourage responsible choices
- be sensitive to sensitive areas
- encourage and support

As they pass through adolescence one can expect alternating times of calm and conflict. Each time a young person is prompted by a new opportunity to become more independent they may experience a surge of enthusiasm or excitement. Since they are facing a new and unfamiliar challenge, they may also feel afraid or overwhelmed. When this happens they may temporarily turn back to the old ways they used to cope as children. They may pout or throw a tantrum to get their way or express frustration. They may withdraw and retreat or want someone to indulge, protect or comfort them. Just as toilet-trained children may suddenly lose their bowel and bladder control following the birth of a younger sibling, teenagers too will regress to more childish levels of behaviour under the impact of strains or stresses.

In addition to physical and intellectual growth accompanying teenage years, there are also four psychological processes that account for the emotional growth of adolescents. These are:

- The process of becoming aware that the adolescent is an individual. This may manifest itself as argumentativeness, silence or questioning as they discover who they are.

- Becoming less dependent on others and learning to think for themselves.

- Developing their own uniqueness and individual character; choosing their own clothes, friends, music, hobbies and food and ways of saying 'This is who I am'.

- Pulling together all the physical, intellectual, emotional, social and spiritual growth teenagers have experienced throughout their lives. For teenagers whose lives have been disordered in some way, this pulling together into a relatively stable and enduring personality, ready to take their place in the community as responsible adults is probably the hardest stage to achieve and where the most help will be needed.

Overcoming anxiety and becoming comfortable at a greater emotional distance from adults is one of the major tasks facing adolescents. If this independence is thrust upon young people before they are emotionally ready then anti-social behaviour may be the misunderstood outcome.

As adolescents move toward adulthood they must face new tasks or challenges and will need help to:

- Find ways to reconcile their increasing freedom, independence and feelings of maturity with their desire to be cared for. A young person was deeply upset that her mother had not sent her a birthday card, although only a few weeks previously she had had a violent argument with her mother, walked out and was now living with friends.

- Start growing out of their naive and somewhat self-centred view of life in order to face some of the difficult realities of the world. A young person on a field trip said to the leader of a group of 50 young people *"My mum is very kind. She always makes my bed for me. Will you do it for me?"* The leader's comments were unprintable!

- Integrate their maturing sexual desires and learn to relate to the opposite sex in a more adult manner.

- Make some revisions in the way they perceive themselves and others.

- Undergo some changes in their emotional lives that will enable them to handle their feelings more maturely and feel more content and settled inwardly.

As they progress, the optimism and enthusiasm of early adolescence are likely to be replaced with feelings of discouragement or failure. Finding out that the world is tough, losing childhood innocence, breaking away from their previous life, and comparing themselves to their peers can create a lot of sadness. It can also be a time of anger as they struggle with the conflicting desires of independence and of wanting to belong. Each young person is different and will attempt to cope differently. They may throw themselves completely into activities so that they do not have to think about important matters. They may become loud, tough or boisterous. Others, looking for security, may throw themselves into a close relationship with someone from the opposite sex or into very intense relationships with their peers.

Facing reality is another difficulty to be overcome by adolescents who may be lacking in both self-awareness and sensitivity to other people.

'Internalization is the process of taking into one's own personality the attitudes, values and characteristics of key people in one's life.' (*Parenting Teens*). It is therefore exceptionally important that young people have adults around them who can influence them appropriately without subsuming them into their beliefs and values.

Adolescents need to:

- develop their own distinct identity and sense of uniqueness and individuality
- progressively separate themselves from their childhood dependency on others
- develop meaningful relationships with peers and others
- crystalise their sexual identity and develop their capacity to relate well to others
- gain confidence and skills to prepare for a career, economic independence and adult responsibilities
- fashion their values, beliefs and attitude toward life.

But they often want the privileges of adulthood without the responsibilities!

Teenagers also need to:

- become comfortable with their feelings, both positive and negative
- become less troubled by strong feelings of love and happiness as well as intense feelings of fear, discouragement and anger

- learn that strong and even conflicting emotions can exist together without causing damage
- find out they can love someone and be angry at them.

Early adolescents, for example, may angrily announce: *"I hate him. I never want to see him again."* Older adolescents may be more able to admit: *"I love her and hate her. She makes me so mad"* or *"I wish I didn't like him."*

Adolescents need to develop clear boundaries between their own thoughts and feelings and the thoughts and feelings of others. They also need to learn how to communicate both their positive and negative feelings appropriately. They need to move beyond temper tantrums, fits of anger and depressed withdrawal so they can communicate their fears and angers and happiness more directly and maturely. A young girl who had spent a good deal of her life in a children's home was placed in a foster home to prepare her for transition to adulthood. Whilst at the foster placement the teenager behaved very well, integrated with the carer's other children and was attending school regularly. However, when alone with the social worker she behaved abominably. After this had happened twice, the carer spoke to the girl about a whole range of issues including acceptable behaviour and discussing problems. Eventually it transpired that although the girl realised she would never be able to live with her parents she would really like to see them. She did not know how to ask her social worker, thought she might be ridiculed or refused, and so had reverted to the only behaviour she knew.

There is no such thing as a 'normal' adolescent but some of the following characteristics may be displayed at different times during a young person's adolescence:

- increased aggressiveness
- more direct expression of their own opinions about clothes, entertainment, politics, activities etc.
- forgetting to do chores or take their responsibilities seriously
- complaining about chores and other activities
- messing about or being silly, especially in front of friends
- making decisions which they know will cause disagreement
- keeping secrets

- stubbornness
- periods of critical or condemning attitude towards anyone in authority.

Many young people may also exhibit any or all of the following:
- chronic irritability and negativism
- rebellion or defiance
- 'don't care' attitude
- an inability to work co-operatively, even with their peers
- frequent depression or outbursts of rage
- prolonged anger.

A very caring highly intelligent colleague was most distraught when his teenage sons consistently belittled him, perpetually implying that he was totally useless – Mark Twain seems to have adequately articulated the conflicts young people feel when they are trying to come to terms with the changes in their lives:

> *"It was a very curious thing. When I was about thirteen my father's intelligence started to drop. His mental abilities continued to decline until I reached twenty-one when these abilities began miraculously to improve."* (unknown source).

The way we treat young people inevitably influences how they will respond to us. Young people do not like being treated differently just because they are young. They will usually respond well to being treated with courtesy, respect and goodwill.

Chapter 3

Adolescents

A brainstorming session on what would be useful to help young people achieve successful lives produced the following headings:

- rights
- equality
- skills: practical/emotional/physical and intellectual
- good health and advice
- caring for themselves and the community and having someone to care for and about them
- advocacy
- access to wide variety of facilities
- pleasant environment
- understanding and setting standards
- ways of coping with conflict
- ability to have fun and enjoy free time
- protection

Research

Recent research carried out by Ann Buchanan and JoAnn Ten Brinke *What Happened When they Were Grown Up? Outcomes from Parenting Experiences*, University of Oxford/Joseph Rowntree highlights:

- young people may need support within their family
- if a young person can be helped to cope when there is conflict within the family then they are less likely to have lasting side effects from divorce or separation, for example

- the emotional needs of young people experiencing family disruption are often unmet and counselling services should be provided
- experience of being 'in care' was a risk factor for high maladjustment at 16
- a small number of young people are at risk of suffering from mental health problems later in life. If adolescents could learn to find 'buffers' to protect them or ways of resolving difficulties this would have a major impact on their adult mental health
- many young people need help to improve their verbal, literacy and academic skills
- there was a direct correlation between the life satisfaction of the research participants at 33 and the extent of the control that they had on their lives at 16.

From this study then, it would appear that if by the time adolescents are 16 years old certain things can be changed in their lives, then when they are 33 they will have achieved life satisfaction, which must be a success in any sense of the word.

Helping young people achieve successful lives

So how can this be achieved? The first part of the chapter looks at some of the areas brainstormed and gives pointers for young people. Other points are covered elsewhere in the book. The second part is entitled 'Making changes' and gives suggestions for helping young people plan for their future and develop the necessary life skills for success.

Rights

Although the European Convention on Human Rights is about to become part of the domestic law in the UK there is concern that this is not sufficiently 'child' orientated to fully implement the UN Convention. As was noted in Children UK 1997 by Gerison Lansdown, Director of the Children's Rights Office *"It is a step in the right direction, but for children, it is not enough. We must welcome this commitment ... but we must also continue to argue for a commitment to full implementation of all the principles of the UN Convention."*

Save the Children's overall approach to young people's rights is to start working with them on what they themselves want, building on their strengths so that they feel valued and respected and can make an active contribution rather than be passive recipients of services.

In order that young people may fully develop they need:

- opportunities to receive information
- to learn skills of expressing opinion
- freedom of thought
- to meet with others
- privacy
- the best possible health and care
- education
- participation in decision making
- protection from exploitation.

Equality

Everyone, regardless of their age, gender, disability, race, ethnic origin, nationality, sexual orientation, social class, religion or language should be treated as equal. Equality in treatment, opportunities and access to services.

Skills

In order to ensure that young people are able to benefit from this equality they need a wide variety of skills:

Practical skills

They need not only educational and life skills, but making and keeping friends, education for free time, coping alone, parenting, housekeeping and budgeting skills in addition to learning about morals, ethics and acceptable standards of behaviour.

Communication and decision making

The chapter on Successful communication offers the adult many suggestions for improving communication with young people and these skills, in turn, are appropriate for helping the adolescents themselves. Decision making is covered later in this chapter.

Coping strategies

One suggestion is setting up mediation schemes whereby young people who are nominated by their peer group learn to act as mediators working together to find solutions to problems such as bullying, graffiti or disruptive behaviour. Another idea is to play communication games, for example, encouraging young people to look at positive things about each other and talking about feelings and emotions.

Fashion and the media

Young people need to learn to not be manipulated by what they hear, see and read but to be able to make decisions and to understand what is right and best for them.

Environment and facilities

Adolescents have a right to a clean, tidy and pleasant environment which is not second best. There may be a dilemma for adults who visit a young person's home and see that the environment may be a health hazard. Do they do nothing or do they take the matter further? Discussing this with a superior may be necessary in order to decide on the family's right to privacy compared with the young person's right to a safe environment.

Health

The Department of Health have set 'health of the young nation' targets which they hope will be achieved by the millennium. The ones that relate to adolescents are:

HIV and sexual health

Cut the pregnancy rate in under 16s by 50% – from 9.5 per 1000 girls aged 13-15 in 1989 to no more than 4.8. Pregnancy during the teens has a higher rate of prematurity and there is also a wide range of socio-economic consequences.

Reduce the proportion of drug users sharing needles from 20%, in 1990 to 5%.

Mental health

Cut the overall suicide rate by 15% from 11.1 per 100,000 population in 1990 to no more than 9.4. There has been a steady rise in male adolescent suicides over the last 10 years.

Cardiovascular disease

Cut the smoking rate of 11-15-year-olds by 33% from 8% to 6%.
Something like 90% of all current regular smokers began smoking before
the age of 16 and as tobacco is as addictive as heroin concentrating on
preventing young people from experimenting with smoking is all-important.

**Cut the calorie intake from fat in the diet from 40%, to below 35%, of
total calorie intake.** Eating habits are embedded even as far back as the
womb with the result that high cholesterol is laid down in the coronary
arteries from an early age.

Cut alcohol intake – adult males to 28 units a week and females 21.
Specific targets for adolescents were not available so the Royal College of
General Practitioners suggest that the adult ones should apply.

Physical activity

Although this is highlighted in the prevention of cardiovascular diseases,
there is no definite target at the moment. The aim is to get more young
people active more often. Various suggestions have been made as to how
much exercise is appropriate, for example moderate exercise for 30 minutes
five times a week.

Accidents

**Cut the deaths due to accidents in the under 15s by 33%, – from 6.7 per
100,000 population in 1989 to no more than 4.5.**

**Cut the death rates due to accidents for the 15-24 age group by 25%,
from 23.2 per 100,000 population in 1989 to no more than 17.4.**
Accidents and injuries are the major cause of death in young people and
cause much morbidity.

Cancer

Cut the rate of deaths due to skin cancer. Sun 'know-how' in teenagers
would help with this, as would early diagnosis and referral of skin
malignancies.

In the chapter on Health, the latest research from young people shows that
their idea of health related matters differs widely from that of the
professionals. Clearly there is a lot of work to be done to achieve some or all
of these targets. Better health education is obviously one area where positive
work can take place.

A Drugs 'Tsar' has just been appointed in the UK to look at ways of reducing the supply of drugs and there are many anti-drugs campaigns in operation such as the setting up of a 'youth jury' in South Yorkshire to look at the evidence in their location and then make recommendations to the council as to what should be done to help reduce drug abuse.

A carer said *"inform them about the stuff on the street, let them know, ask them to tell you what they take but let them know you do not approve. Be honest, tell them drugs and solvents can kill."* Adults who take drugs, even socially, may have a problem being quite so dogmatic and must reconcile their own behaviour against that which is best for the young person. What is important is that young people have all the information available and understand the risks and possible dangers. They also have to learn the skill of resisting peer pressure.

Recent research reported in the media, and also that noted by Amanda Sandford (on behalf of 'ASH' in *Children and Smoking*, Highlight, National Children's Bureau), indicates that education on the dangers of smoking and glue sniffing at an early age often does prevent smoking in adulthood. The ASH work also noted that even if young people who received this education did smoke, they often started later and then found it easier to give up.

Many young people who miss out on school miss out on sex education and often have complete misconceptions – *"I couldn't have had sex, I didn't sleep with him." "I can't get raped if I'm wearing a tampon"* may sound incredulous but are both true statements.

Young people who have been abused will invariably have heightened sexual feelings and will need help to understand this. They will also need help to control these desires, to learn what is 'normal' and how to treat other people with respect and dignity. Equally they will need all the emotional support you can give them.

Standards

Young people will tell you that they want to know the difference between right and wrong. They want to be helped to tell the truth and learn how to keep promises. They also want to learn to take responsibility for their own actions and self-discipline, and help those less fortunate and weaker than themselves. They also need help to learn how to act considerately and respect the rights, properties and opinions of others.

The Council for Education in World Citizenship (address at the back of the book) provides resource materials, support, conferences and educational events for young people locally, regionally and nationally on such things as global issues and young people's rights and responsibilities as citizens of tomorrow's interdependent and multicultural world.

Sports/hobbies/having fun

Young people need real opportunities to participate in a wide variety of sports and leisure activities. Participation in sport by adolescents varies in popularity over time. However, many see sport as:

- a way of directing physical energies and aggressiveness
- encouraging self-discipline
- showing dedication
- developing team spirit
- learning responsibility and self-belief
- creating a 'feel good' factor
- understanding fair play
- learning sociability skills
- being healthy.

It can also be fun.

Many of these descriptions could also be used for other activities from bird watching to drama to landscape painting.

Many who do not participate physically in sport are often avid spectators and there is a growing realisation of the importance of the need for fair play and good standards in sport as an example for young people to carry forward into adulthood.

As mentioned under 'Health' above, there are significant long-term health benefits from regular physical activity. Participating in sport would also appear to be a way of preventing crime.

What young people need are opportunities to find out what is possible, to try alternatives, have new experiences and to make choices; in this way they will learn to take responsibility for their own lives. This will hold them in good stead for the future and help them to enjoy their free time.

Conflict resolution and avoidance

The Oxford study showed that young people need help in developing skills to resolve conflict. These skills will not only be useful for conflict between their peers but also for coping with disputes within the family and other adults. The process of conflict resolution may be defined as:

"… bargaining and debate. The bargaining process has been construed in terms of concession making: most of the experimentation has concentrated on factors that influence the amount and rate of concessions made by the bargainers. The process of debate has emphasised the role of verbal behaviour and persuasion in negotiation …" (Conflict Resolution, Theories and Practice, edited by Denis Sandole and Hugo Van der Merwe).

In other words, conflict resolution is a communication process for managing a conflict and negotiating a solution. Resolving conflict to achieve positive outcomes involves defusing the emotional energy and achieving a mutual understanding of similarities and differences. Conflict management is complete when destructive behaviour has been reduced, hostile attitudes lessened and negotiation or problem solving arrives at an outcome that satisfies all parties.

Elsewhere in the book there are examples of skills for adults to use to resolve problems and some of these skills are equally appropriate for use by the young person. However, if the adolescent is to be helped to both understand the reasons for their behaviour and the behaviour of others, then they will need to understand themselves. They will need to learn to:

- own their own emotions
- acknowledge positive intentions
- separate out issues
- listen and reflect
- identify their position and interests and that of others
- negotiate
- be prepared to compromise.

If young people are experiencing conflict within the home, such as parents continually arguing, carrying out the above analysis can be beneficial. They may not be able to do it entirely alone, they may need the help of a trusted adult. They probably cannot influence what is going on around them but by being able to look objectively at themselves they will be better able to detach themselves from the other people's conflict and thus get on with their lives without being overtaken by the stressful situation.

If the conflict directly involves the young person, say they 'hate' a teacher or key worker, there are 4 stages through which to progress:

- **Awareness** – being aware of the negative feelings of the situation.
- **Self-preparation** – (a) separating the people from the problem
  - (b) deciding what outcomes they require
  - (c) understanding the reasons
- **Defusing negative emotions** – each listening to the other person's point of view. This may not bring about a settlement but will at least give an understanding of differences and mutual respect of one another.
- **Negotiation** – enabling each party to achieve a mutually agreed outcome with respect for individual differences.

Most conflict resolution situations require someone to act as a mediator or go between. Much of the self-awareness discussions mentioned later in this chapter are essential for the successful use of conflict management.

By understanding and using this process with the help of adults, a young person may become more confident and better able to resolve possible conflicts before they occur. The very process of listening to the other person's point of view is a huge step in preparation for adulthood. Also, the skills learned will be useful in adulthood in relationships with their partner, family and their own children.

These skills can also be adapted for use when refusing to take drugs, smoke or sniff glue, or generally to withstand peer pressure in other ways. The confidence and coping strategies should enable the adolescent to say 'no' if they so wish.

Depression and distress are other areas where just analysing the assumed problem can certainly lessen the pain and often reduce it altogether if positive alternatives can be found.

Death or separation

This is difficult to cope with for everyone but particularly for adolescents who are simultaneously experiencing other changes in their life. The above may help but other things to consider are:

If you know someone close to the young person is likely to die then it is a good idea to prepare him or her as much as possible. Talk about feelings and emotions, both theirs and the other people involved, how different people will react in different ways. Rituals around death vary depending on the culture or religion and information may be required so the young person can be suitably advised.

When the death occurs they may feel shock, disbelief, numbness, misery, anger, questioning, sadness, self-blame and blame others. Do not let them try to get over these feelings of pain too quickly. There is no set time that bereavement lasts. The pain will recur again and again – at birthdays, anniversaries, Christmas, holiday times and at other times that were special for the particular person.

Sometimes a young person who experiences death will want to be alone, yet not alone – someone whom they can trust should be nearby; they may feel desolation and despair and just want to talk – be there. Others may be angry, and ways to cope with that anger will be required. A 16 year old who lived in a hostel came into school late one day saying that one of the other residents had committed suicide. He was angry. Blaming everyone especially the warden, saying more should have been done. His year tutor invited him to play squash where he ran and ran until he had used up his aggressions. He was then able to talk calmly and rationally about the situation.

Divorce and separation may be very much like death to adolescents in many ways. They often blame themselves. Wherever possible they should be allowed to be involved in discussions about the separation with both parties. A form of grieving may also take place. Be a good listener. Be prepared.

Protection

Some people, either because they misbehaved when they were teenagers or because they are naturally nervous people, attempt to protect adolescents too much, often causing embarrassment in front of friends. Whether you meet the young person from an event, take them in the car, let them walk home alone, or go to nightclubs unaccompanied are all things that should be discussed before conflict occurs. Many young people will say "... *is allowed to* ..." when the friend is actually saying the same thing to his or her parent or carer.

Talk these concerns over and then agree the ground rules, reconciling greater freedom with the risks involved. It may be hard to let go but it really is important for this to happen if a young person is not to go absolutely wild at a later date. Providing they are armed with all the ammunition (figuratively speaking) that you can give them you must trust that they have learned to make their own decisions in life.

Young people who have televisions in their bedrooms have the opportunity to watch TV whenever they wish. This may be a good way of entertaining but it may also be a way of young people experiencing life in a sordid and unacceptable way. Video shops hire out films that are often violent, sexually explicit or give young people a false impression of life. Computer games can offer similar experiences.

Whilst there is very little concrete evidence, it is known that if a young person has a tendency for epileptic fits then TV or computer games may start them off because of what is known as 'flicker fusion'. Violence on screen can produce violent feelings in the same way as very sexually explicit films can heighten the sex drive of viewers. Also young people may have difficulty discerning fact from fiction.

The Internet is another area of concern and *Internet Access Made Easy*, issue 3, October 1997 has given some useful guidelines for surfing the net safely. If you are concerned about young people getting access to offensive material or porn, use a filtering programme. There is also a rating system available on-line. RSAC is the most comprehensive system available at present. It uses four headings; violence, sex, nudity and language and has a 0 – 4 numbering system with 0 being the least offensive. It was originally developed for computer games but is now used quite comprehensively among Web browsers. It is up to whoever is responsible for the young person to ensure appropriate ratings are used. This can also be a topic for discussion.

It has also been discovered that in addition to young people being addicted to computer games there is now an accepted psychological disorder called IAD (Internet Addiction Disorder) for people who cannot stop surfing the net.

Young people need to learn to make informed choices about their viewing and surfing but before they are capable of so doing they will need help, guidance and some control.

Making changes

The aim of anyone working with adolescents should be to help them become:

> *"individuals who can make a meaningful contribution to shaping their own lives and the life of the community in which they live"* (anon).

One suggestion for helping young people achieve this 'meaningful contribution' is for them to develop their own life plan (see p.22). The source of these eight steps is Judy Tame, *Life Planning for Executives, Long Range Planning*, Vol.26, no.5, October 1993, reproduced with kind permission from Elsevier Science Ltd, The Boulevard, Langford Lane, Kidlington, Oxford OX5 1GB, UK.

It is important to remember that answering these questions is not the end, more part of a continuous process. It would be useful to go over it say in three months' time and discuss any changes and their reasons. Gradually, young people could do their own life plan, if they wish, either alone, or with friends.

Note that **having** is an objective, whereas the life goal is about **being and doing**.

Acquiring money is a means to an end and hence an objective, but unlikely to be a satisfying end in itself.

Whilst producing this life plan or in other work with young people it may become apparent that they need help in other areas of their personal development which are included in the following pages.

Life plan

Step	Examples	Time frame
Diagnosis	Who are you? What is important to you? What are your attributes? What are your aspirations?	Past and present
Values	What is more/less important to you? What cannot you live without?	
Personal mission/ purpose	What do you have to offer? What do you believe in?	
Life goals	What do you want to do? What do you want to create? What do you want to experience? What do you want to be?	Long-term – may not be dateable
Resources	Strengths Talents Skills Experience Knowledge Relationships Finances	Medium-term – 6 months +
Objectives	Career Family Financial Education/training Health/fitness etc.	
Next steps	Speak to... Write to... Talk to... Decide on... Ask...	Short-term – now to 6 months
Review	What worked/did not work? What did you learn? How have you changed?	3/6/12 months

Personality development

The remainder of this chapter identifies a range of common feelings and experiences so young people will be able to better recognise and express their own feelings and develop their personality.

A few trigger words are included. Some activities suggest young people write things down. This is not necessary. It may be equally valuable, and sometimes more successful, for discussion to take place. Alternatively, young people could tape record what they say, listen to it again later and talk it over with their friends or friendly adults.

Feelings and emotions

– delighted	– in a rage
– nervous	– violent
– agitated	– full of joy
– volatile	– strengthened
– explosive	– maintained
– uptight	– express feelings
– furious	– deepen
– terrified	– terminate
– frightened	– be open
– thrilled	– share
– sad	– separation
– glad	– painful
– hurt	– hurting
– mad	– working at
– happy	– nurturing
– ill	– loving
– angry	– caring

- For early adolescents working in a group or individually you could have a series of faces cut out from coloured magazines. Get young people to write down or call out what emotions they think these people are experiencing. Discussion on circumstances, reasons for these feelings or other ways of expression may well lead to discussion on young people's own feelings.

- Ask young people to write down/call out/talk about words relating to their emotions now and in the past, talk about examples and reasons why.

- Discuss which feelings words such as boredom, anger, terror create in them and others, and why.

- Where and when particular emotions occur is another topic for discussion, and then the reason why e.g. how colours affect people – 'ratty red' or 'dreary grey'; plants, tidiness, a particular teacher. Fast food restaurants are an example where bright colours dominate in order to encourage customers to eat up, drink up and move on.

- Watching videos or TV films together and then discussing both content and how 'we felt' is appropriate for all age groups.

When exploring emotions and feelings, it is important to realise that there is a danger that something is said which may trigger feelings of real sadness or anger. Be prepared with an action plan of how to cope with the particular young person, and others in a group if doing group work.

Discussing emotions alone may well not be sufficient but is a very good starting point. Coping strategies may also need to be introduced such as taking up a physical sport to relieve pent up aggression, decorating a room, taking up painting, listening to quiet music.

Critical thinking and decision making

– what's best	– perceptive
– choices	– choosing
– weighing up	– looking behind
– think about	– reflect
	→

- predict
- decisions
- outcomes
- advantages
- disadvantages
- what will happen
- confusing
- consequences

- taking responsibility
- image
- assessing
- work it out
- critical thinking
- conflict
- conflicting messages

Help young people to be in situations where each day they have to make decisions. For busy adults it is often easier to do tasks or decide themselves rather than spend time enabling children and young people to make their own decisions. Decision making then is not an integral part of adolescents' lives so when they do have to make decisions this can be quite a shock and a difficult transition.

Learning to co-operate/working as a group/making and keeping friends

- working together
- two heads are better than one
- alone
- individually
- co-operating
- part of the group
- isolated
- on one's own
- caring and sharing

- building together
- trust
- support
- one of a team
- friendship
- helpful
- strengthened
- maintained
- express feelings

- deepen
- terminate
- be open
- share
- separation
- painful
- hurting
- working at
- nurturing
- loving
- caring
- other people's point of view

Young people change emotionally, physically and intellectually during adolescence. This may make coping with relationships difficult. Joining clubs or teams is one obvious solution. It also helps to realise that a young person may suddenly want to leave a group. It is important to discuss the motives and possible methods for so doing and why this is better than the teenager just not turning up.

Many young people will tell you they have 'loads of friends' when in actual fact these people are only acquaintances. Understanding the concept and responsibilities of true friendship is also important. Many teenage girls become dependent on boyfriends who often do not treat them too well. Everyone needs opportunities to meet a wide variety of people, old, young, different sex, disabled and able bodied and to learn to both respect and be respected in social situations.

If they learn to work and co-operate with others when they move to another location they will be better prepared to make new friends and avoid loneliness and isolation.

An activity might be to ask either a group, or an individual, to write down the name of their best friends a year ago and then now. With them compare these lists and talk about the reasons for the changes. If they say they have no friends, ask them to describe a friend they would like to have so you can think about ways to help them build friendships.

The uniqueness of me

- skills
- limitations
- aspirations
- hopes
- unique
- special

- different
- similarities
- a rarity
- unusual
- self-value

Young people could draw up a list or chart on what they could do, say five years ago, now and what they hope to be able to do in five years time. They could then do a similar thing but make a list under 'I can', 'I can't', 'I will'. This is useful for both individual and group work.

Building self-confidence

- ambition
- affirming
- personal goals
- improving
- setting targets
- aims
- aspirations
- getting better

- developing
- encouragement
- positive
- negative
- constructive
- destructive
- building up

The best way to achieve this is to help young people to:
- find out about themselves
- explore what they can and cannot do

- recognise their limitations in a positive way
- set goals for the future
- understand the effect their actions can have on other people
- examine how other people may affect their own self-confidence.

Eating disorders, for example, emanate from low self-esteem.

Young girls often see motherhood as something they **can** achieve when they think they can achieve very little else.

Values

– bullying	– sexuality
– cheating	– divorce
– deceit	– the truth
– cruelty	– promises
– prejudice	– respect
– discrimination	– swearing
– sexism	– religion
– abortion	– 'grassing'
– loyalty	

"I want to know right from wrong" said a Hampshire teenager. We get our set of values of life as we grow up. Some we get from family, some we get at school, some we learn at play and others we learn from friends and other people who influence us. Some people get their set of values from their religion. Other people may share these values, have no religion but still may be very good people.

One should be aware how easy it may be to influence young people as they develop their own set of values and should be wary of imposing one's own values on a young person. However, it is important that young people learn about:

- right and wrong
- telling the truth
- keeping promises
- citizenship
- respect both of people and other people's property
- acting considerately
- helping those less fortunate and weaker than themselves
- taking personal responsibility for their actions and self-discipline

Decision making

– ideas	– why did it happen?
– judgements	– what might happen if ...?
– observations	– if I do that then ...?
– the evidence	– what am I trying to achieve?
– freedom	– what are the alternatives?
– effect on other people	– choices
– what's best?	

To make decisions young people need to have opportunities to make decisions and to learn to think about the situation, take it steady, not rush, think about other ideas, weigh up the possibilities, think about what might happen, sift and organise the facts and information they have; if possible, experiment and then decide.

They also need support if the decision made turns out to be wrong; to understand that it may be better to have made a decision than to not have made one at all. They will also need to learn from the experience and to be encouraged to try again. If they have been encouraged to make a decision it will increase their sense of 'ownership' of their life and thus increase their self-esteem at the same time.

If we really want to achieve success with young people then it is important that they should learn to be responsible for their own destiny. However, young people need adults to help them to develop the necessary skills, to be a role model, mediator, confidant and friend.

Chapter 4

The adult

Creating a positive attitude

This chapter is about creating a positive attitude for those working with adolescents. Confidence is the key to success. This means having positive feelings about young people and also having positive feelings about yourself. The first part of the chapter gives practical ideas and explanations which will help create the right atmosphere and the second part is about caring for yourself.

When a wide cross-section of young people were asked 'what makes a good … carer/teacher/youth worker/social worker', the following answers were remarkably similar regardless of the profession to which they were referring:

– polite	– laughs
– fair	– knows what's on your mind
– understands you	– you know what they think
– strict	– they ask what you think
– interesting	– respects you
– kind	– makes you feel welcome
– caring	– comes on time
– gives you confidence	– explains what they do
– not too involved	– explains what is going on
– talks to you	– keeps promises
– listens	– follows up

A very experienced foster carer, when referring to the Guardian ad Litem service made a very poignant observation:

*"15 minutes of special time is worth much more than 3 hours of graft. If GAL doesn't make an impact in the first 10 minutes – they've lost it. **It's the same as all work with young people, you must be prepared.**"*

In *Getting Started Topic 1* by Wendy Rogers et al., The Open University it is suggested that those working with young people need to have skills such as:

- **empathy**, the ability to focus on and gain an insight into how the other person is feeling as well as how they see the world
- **listening and responding** positively to what the young person has to say by testing out ideas, perceptions, options for action
- **building trust** by establishing confidence and respect between the adult and the young person through the development of effective forms of communication
- **valuing** the young person for who they are, as well as valuing differences in lifestyle, culture and need.

A care worker was being interviewed for work involving carrying out research to elicit the views of young people 'in care' in different parts of the country. During the interview she was given a scenario and asked how she would cope. Unhesitatingly she gave a description of how she would physically manhandle the young person. The reply to further questioning on what she would do next related to locking up the young person, place of safety etc.. It was obvious that this person had received no training in working with young people; had not thought about the types of situation she might be in during the research and that at no time had the question of relationships, respect or understanding crossed her mind.

Training needs

So what training might have been helpful to her and might help others working with adolescence?

Knowledge
By understanding the way young people think, why they behave the way they do, which areas will help them develop then confrontation will be avoided.

Know yourself
Another important area of knowledge is to know yourself, your strengths
and weaknesses. When I first went into teaching, working with 15-16 year
olds in an inner city multi-racial school, I was constantly given the advice
"start tough and then ease off later". That was the worst advice I have ever been
given.

My first day of teaching was a slanging match between me and a variety of
young people shouting at each other – often the only response young
people know and use. That evening I decided I would either be myself or
give up teaching. My way is quite casual, friendly, using humour (not
sarcasm), respect, individuality and consultation. In over 20 years I think I
shouted three times and the absolute silence that followed was amazing. I
had always explained that I was like *'the little girl with a curl down the middle
of her forehead – when she was good she was very very good and when she was bad
she was horrid'*. Shouting only heightens tensions and makes matters worse
and can only ever be a short-term hard earned solution.

That is not to say there was never confrontation. On one occasion a lad with
a history of violence was playing pool and was asked to put the balls away
whilst he was still holding the cue. He refused and was verbally aggressive.
Slowly, quietly and patiently the teacher talked to him, waiting until the rest
of the group had moved away so he would not lose face. He put the balls
away. However, the next day, because he was asked in an aggressive way by a
different teacher he lashed out with the cue and was expelled.

Adults also need to come to terms with their own beliefs, feelings, emotions
and prejudices in order to avoid prejudging young people.

Communication
There is a wide variety of communication skills that can assist in creating the
right atmosphere for working with adolescents in the chapter on Successful
Communication. However, a few are summarised below:

Body language
It is important to know that the way you behave, your body language and
demeanour will affect adolescents. An independent visitor (IR) was at a
secure unit and asked to see a 13 year old called Chris who had arrived

recently from Wales. She was told that he was misbehaving and acting aggressively so it wasn't possible. She offered to wait and requested that the lad be told that she was there and would like to see him.

Chris asked to see the visitor so she went into the room where the assistant manager was standing, arms folded, head held aloof whilst Chris was slumped against the wall. The IR asked the manager to leave and promptly told Chris that she was going to sit on the floor (there was no furniture in the room) and invited him to sit down too which he did quite soon after. A long conversation ensued between crying sessions and Chris highlighted some of his grievances. The manager eventually was asked to come back so the IR could speak on Chris's behalf. He immediately folded his arms, stood aloof and spoke in a superior manner to Chris who soon became aggressive and uncompromising again.

Unfortunately the IR had no authority over the manager but the episode was mentioned at the review meeting the following week.

Where you stand/sit
This is also significant. If you are addressing a group, ensure the sun is not on your back and thus shining in the eyes of the young people. Don't always stand in the same place, move about – you'll get a different perspective of the group, give the young people a different back drop to look at and also you will be able to see the responses of different people in the group.

Hands in the pockets signify a casual approach and there may be a danger that you will not be taken seriously. If you want young people to learn standards then you have to set them.

Attitudes
The way you walk, dress, speak, your mannerisms or personal hygiene may send out the wrong messages – *"you could fry an egg on her hair, it's so greasy"*, *"I'm not having anything to do with him – he stinks"*, *"fancy dressing like that, she thinks she's 16 when she's 60"* are self explanatory comments.

It is important to remember that adolescents will think that whoever is working with them is very old. When they meet the person years later they often say *"you haven't changed"* or *"you don't look a day older"*. Although that may be good for the ego, it is not really true, just that their perspectives have changed. Young people do not like those working with them to be too 'chummy' or 'pally'. They want someone to be their friend, but a friend from a distance. It is also difficult if you are too 'matey' when you need to take disciplinary action.

> *"Just allowing that somebody may experience life differently from you is not much help if you do not use this to begin to see the world from their perspective and then consider how you can offer positive forms of support, guidance and encouragement."* (World of Difference, Notes on Disability)

Promises

Never make promises which cannot be kept. Quite often it's easier to say *'may be'*, *'I'll try'*, *'I'll find out'*, *'probably'* than actually saying *'no'* with all the consequences that might mean. If you want to avoid the young people feeling let down, then the truth, put tactfully and carefully is far better.

The culture and ethos of the establishment

All organisations have their own culture but sometimes this culture has been allowed to develop over time in such a way that is to the detriment of the young people for whom it was intended to serve and help. The following are actual examples where the people involved were more interested in their own well-being than that of the young people. In all cases, it had gone on for so long that it was an accepted albeit unethical part of the establishment.

The manager of a certain retailer in a market town each Saturday evening delivered to the local children's home, cakes and pastries which had reached their sell-by date. He obviously assumed that these would be given to the residents. Unfortunately staff took the cakes and pastries home and the young people hardly ever saw them. The manager of the children's home was asked about this and his reply was that there was nothing that could be done. Apparently it had gone on for so long that staff saw it as 'perks' of the job. This only became known publicly when one of the residents was fostered by a member of staff and she was given the food. She officially complained.

Not long afterwards, a similar perk came to light. A major chain store in an inner city area had clothes which had been returned as faulty to the store. These were then delivered regularly to the local children's home. Here the staff chose the best and then let the young people choose from that which was remaining.

Towards the end of the day on a school trip to Wimbledon the PE staff member who had organised the visit called the staff together. She said there was £x for staff to have a drink. This money was left over from the fees collected from the young people for the visit. When challenged it transpired that this was usual practice. Since then young people have confirmed that they had always suspected as much.

In many schools, children's homes and secure units staff are known to run their own businesses when they should be working with adolescents, yet no one seems willing to do anything to put a stop to it. Recent cases of paedophilia and child abuse have particularly heightened the need for staff to be vigilant at all times and to be willing to take action.

To earn the respect of young people it is necessary to:

- set standards even if this results in unpopularity
- be willing to stand up and object
- make representations
- put the rights of the young people first.

How can anyone respect staff who behave in that or similar ways?

"Don't do as I do, do as I say" is a dreadful attitude and one very likely to cause problems, for instance, a no smoking rule. In a secure unit smoking was banned for everyone under 16 years, which for many residents was extremely difficult as they had probably been smoking since they were 11 or 12 years old. Staff and older young people had a room adjacent to the main lounge in which they were allowed to smoke. This room had an extractor fan and the door was meant to be kept closed. This was a dubious decision which was abused. Staff regularly lit up their cigarette in the room and either left the door open or smoked in the lounge. The tobacco smell caused all sorts of problems for the young people and heightened tensions which often led to aggressive behaviour.

Assessments, files and reports

What is written can have a bearing on young people for the rest of their lives. Written records can not only scar or upset a young person, those records go with them for ever. Subjective comments should be avoided. Written records should not be left lying around or within easy access on a computer. Confidentiality should be ensured at all times.

Research

It is often stated that not enough notice is taken of research. Research can often **and should** inform practice. For example, research by Lesley Saunders and Bob Broad of De Montfort University looked at the health needs of young people leaving care. These results have major implications for all those working with adolescents.

Working with parents

It is over 20 years since schools realised that if they wanted to truly work with parents then they had to organise many of their meetings in the evening. Other professions have been slow to follow and still organise meetings during the day which means that parents either have to take time off work, often losing pay, or cannot attend. The whole ethos of working in partnership with parents needs to be re-examined and Chapter 5 gives some thoughts and practical suggestions.

Coping strategies

Young people will, of course, not always behave the way you want them to or you think they should. There are a variety of strategies available; some will be easy to implement, others will require practice. Some will work for one person and not another. What is important is to have different strategies to hand in case of need.

Building relationships

The chapters on Promoting equality, the Law, Health and Education have been included to give background information. It may be something to look at/discuss together, either in time of need or as a general topic. Some other topics might be the concept of power, citizenship and the participation and involvement of young people in decision making.

Education

Young people's attitude to education during adolescence is either incredibly intense to the extreme but more often than not it is disinterested, insulting and outright hostile. The Education chapter offers some alternative strategies for improving a young person's attitude and educational achievement.

Practical suggestions for working with young people

Young people:
- be proud
- only accept the best
- be on the side of the young person
- advocate
- explain what is going on
- consult
- discuss
- don't punish everyone unless you are absolutely sure everyone is to blame, not just because you can't find the culprit
- compliment the young people, say how nice they look when they smile
- thank them when they are helpful
- make them feel welcome
- help them to have a positive attitude
- many young people you work with are the product of poor parenting; don't punish the young people because of this

Adults and the young people:
- set clear boundaries
- make the young people feel good about themselves
- explain to the young people what you are doing/expect/would like
- let young people know you will stick your neck out for them, that you will not let them down. Help them to understand that in return they shouldn't let you down.
- say '*thank you*'
- acknowledge achievements, no matter how small
- don't talk **at**, talk **to** young people

Adults and themselves:
- be punctual
- avoid irritating habits
- don't gossip
- you may have to occasionally 'bend' the rules
- always have something else ready that you can use if what you planned doesn't work out
- be prepared
- say it and mean it
- make sure any materials you use are fresh, up-to-date, not last years or dog eared
- set standards, don't say *'that'll do'*, either it is up to standard or not
- make the place look good, put up some pictures, have some plants around
- adults don't always know best
- sometimes young people may come to apologise, give them a chance to speak
- don't leave keys in the doors of rooms or walk-in cupboards; you may get locked in!
- don't put temptation in a teenager's way by leaving valuables lying around

- For your own safety, remember you may be vulnerable, know your organisation's policy on punishment and restraint.
- Beware of corners of rooms or between large pieces of furniture as you may get trapped by a young person or a group.
- Don't flirt or allow yourself to be taken in by young people flirting with you.
- Some young people may appear to be articulate, confident, well behaved and so may not get the attention they deserve.

If you want young people to respect you then you have to respect them.

Caring for yourself

Caring for yourself is probably in many ways the most important part of the book. Working with adolescents can be stressful, exhausting and thankless. Coping strategies are needed; support networks put in place and an understanding of self is required. This is not just for self-preservation, which is important in itself, but also because to be successful with a young person it is necessary to feel good about yourself.

The following are suggestions other professionals have given:

- if you feel you need counselling then ask for it
- keep a diary – use it as a therapeutic dustbin, for reflection, where you went wrong
- practise what you preach
- take a break
- spend time doing what you want to do
- have a way forward
- it's OK to cry
- it's OK to admit you did things wrong
- apologise to the young person, tell them that at the time you thought it was right
- accept that people will criticise but it still hurts
- understand your own feelings
- feel safe to say "I trust you, but I don't know why"
- absorb negatives
- have someone you can speak to at the end of a telephone
- make a note of things you want to talk over
- you can't do everything on your own
- be a team player, but understand you'll get hurt if the team deserts or lets you down, it's the same as with young people
- beware of alcohol – it's the easy way and doesn't last
- understand that you may hide behind humour or pretend everything is fine.

If you have had to intervene or had a problem with a young person then afterwards it is important that your own personal responses are considered.

The emotional health of those working with young people who have persistently misbehaved must be paramount. Working with distressed and disturbed young people can in itself, be distressing and disturbing. Traditionally we have been good at addressing the young peoples' needs, but less good at considering the emotional needs of those working with them.

Consider the situation where you have been asked to work with a difficult group of young people with whom you are not familiar. The situation goes badly for several weeks despite your best efforts and ends with a major confrontation with a difficult teenager. What do you think the immediate effects of such an incident on you might be? Experience, and research, suggests you are likely to feel anger, biological changes – increased heart rate, tense muscles, fast breathing, raised blood pressure and behavioural changes – talking over fast and loud, agitation, moving around more than normal.

The effect may not end here, although individuals are, of course, extremely variable in their responses. Again research indicates that for some time after a traumatic incident you are likely to feel increased physical tension, psychological numbing and physical exhaustion. These are not signs of weakness but normal and natural human responses to traumatic events. We also know that, if an individual is exposed to such a situation over long periods of time, the typical effects might be:

- depression
- feelings of hopelessness
- guilt – over problems that occur
- loss of confidence – in your skills
- loss of vocation
- over-estimation of the risk of future violence
- apprehension
- anger.

Anger accumulates over time and can easily be displaced, on to family and friends.

If such feelings go unacknowledged and are not dealt with, your emotional health is at risk. You should consider:

- **Immediate and personal feelings** – developing one's own personal strategies for dealing with the immediate emotional impact of the crisis; seeking out a trusted friend or colleague for support.

- **Staff support systems** – there should be opportunities to discuss difficult situations in regular staff group meetings, formal and informal de-briefing after incidents, documenting problems in order to inform changes in procedures that might need to be made; responsive support to provide practical ideas for managing the situation better.

- **Awareness** – being aware that there will be some negative response from others; that it is common for self blame to occur and that reaction to a particular situation will be much affected by one's own prevailing mood.

It is also important to realise that certain situations can cause pressures on staff. These might be coming face to face with the destructive effects of racism, sexism, ageism and so on and realising that the young person may be going through similar situations as yourself. This can bring back painful memories.

Neil Thompson, Michael Murphy and Steve Stradling published an article in *Child Care Forum*, issue 26, September 1997 offering ten guidelines for dealing with everyday pressures in childcare work which they feel will better equip staff for dealing with the challenges presented by stress in a demanding occupation. These are reproduced here as they equally apply to those working with adolescents:

---

1.   **Know your enemy** – What is it about your job, or about your life more generally that leads to stress? It helps to know what it is that makes pressure just that bit too much and therefore translates it into harmful stress. You don't need to psycho-analyse yourself, but it does pay dividends to know what your stress factors are so that you can avoid or control them.

→

---

2.   **Be clear about what helps you cope** – We all have different strategies for coping. What are yours? What is it that helps you keep your head above water? Make a list of these (either on your own or with a friend/partner) and look at how you can strengthen or extend them. The greater the coping resources you can draw on, the less likely it is that you will experience stress. Also we must be wary of the tendency to become too dependent on a small number of coping resources, leaving us vulnerable if circumstances conspire to deprive us of one or more of these.

3.   **Identify your support systems and use them** – Support is available from various quarters but there are often two problems associated with this: people don't know what support is available; and they feel uneasy about using it – not realising that asking for help when needed is a sign of strength, not weakness. In order to be able to invest in clients we also need to invest in ourselves. The more people find out about what help is available and use it, the sooner these myths about weakness will be dispelled.

4.   **Take a step back** – From time to time it pays to step back and review where you are up to in your life. How are things working out? Are you getting where you want to go? What steps do you need to take to change things for the better? This sort of review helps to give us a sense of control and confidence, important factors in tackling stress.

5.   **Be clear about your responsibilities** – You have to know the difference between what is your responsibility and what is not. If you fail to meet your responsibilities there can be very stressful consequences. However, it also applies the other way round – if you take responsibility for something that is not down to you, then you are inviting additional unnecessary pressures. The line between your responsibility and someone else's is an important one to draw.

→

6. **Be realistic** – There is only so much one person can achieve. It is therefore important that we recognise our limitations and avoid the harmful trap of having unrealistic expectations about what we can achieve. We have to accept that there are some problems that cannot be solved, some goals that cannot be reached.

7. **Collect your rewards** – Childcare work involves both pressures and rewards. It is easy to get bogged down in the problems and pressures, and lose sight of the rewards and satisfactions. A negative, overly cynical approach is potentially very destructive – we have to maintain the balance by recognising the positives, and occasionally celebrating a piece of work well done.

8. **Work together** – Collaborating on particular projects or working together as part of a team more generally can bring tensions and problems. However it can also bring considerable rewards, not least in the form of a tremendous source of support. There is a lot to be gained from working together and supporting each other.

9. **Keep a clear focus** – Pressure of work can often mean that we lose sight of what we are trying to achieve. We 'drift' and lose our focus. This can be the beginning of a vicious circle in which the lack of focus causes stress but then makes us less well-equipped to deal with that stress. It therefore pays to keep a clear focus at all times on what we are doing and why we are doing it.

10. **Get a life!** – Childcare work is often difficult and demanding, and brings with it many tensions and pressures. However there is more to life than work. Although it can feel uncomfortably like being selfish we are unlikely to be able to care effectively for others if we do not care for ourselves.

These are not guaranteed solutions, nor do they form an exhaustive list. They should, however, provide a useful starting point for developing the necessary skills and strategies for keeping stress in check. Making changes in our lives to reduce stressors and increase coping resources can be painful in the short-term, but can have a powerfully positive effect in our long-term battle against stress.

The conclusion of this chapter then is that if you remember and implement the first part of this chapter then the second part will not be so important. However, realistically, it really is important that you care for yourself and care for young people in equal proportions.

Chapter 5

Working with parents

This chapter starts by discussing, in general terms, parents' attitudes to adolescence. It continues with early intervention; this comprises a range of strategies intended to prevent or mitigate later adverse situations. Then it highlights the latest research findings regarding parents as noted in The Joseph Rowntree Social Policy Research Findings no. 106 dated October 1996. The conclusions from this report have wide implications for those working with parents. The chapter then goes on to explore ideas for working with parents and concludes with specific ideas and suggestions for success.

Working with parents can be double-edged. By just talking to the family or being there and listening, the stress of a situation can be eased. On the other hand, working with parents can look at strategies such as coping with conflict, managing difficult behaviour, and understanding adolescence. It can mean different things at different times to different people.

Parenting adolescents

One of the first things that will be needed when working with parents is to find out:

- what is the parenting ethos?
- what are their expectations?
- what do they see as being their responsibility?

Many parents feel that once their children become adolescents they cease being children who need help and guidance to become adults. More, they see them as sophisticated and worldly-wise in matters of sex, drugs, music, computers and consumerism. Sadly, many young people are not ready for this withdrawal of parental support and are unable to withstand peer pressure to conform.

In previous generations, parents did not expect teenagers to behave like adults so they tolerated teenage awkwardness, rebelliousness, mood swings and social gaffes. They also felt able to provide guidelines and standards to help adolescents to establish their own limits, values and self-identity.

Whilst adolescents are sophisticated in some respects, they are quite naïve in others. However, this sophisticated perception has led parents to abandon much responsibility previously provided. There is also less tolerance and parents and society generally are often critical and disapproving of adolescence. Many parents also feel liberated once their children become adolescents. They think that overnight a young person is suddenly able to fend for his or herself. In reality, young people still need a protected time within which to adjust. They still need the security of adult role models who can provide guidelines and support.

When discussing parental attitudes recently a colleague became quite distressed. She said *"When Andy was 16 and kicking over the traces, I thought that provided I gave him food, clothing and shelter, he would be happy, and anyway I was busy getting on with my own life. Eventually he left and went to live with his father – I thought he would soon come back, but he did not. Now 24, he has told me that what he hated most when he was 16 was that I wasn't there."*

Another instance was when a young lad was returning home from school late after a sports match. He turned to the teacher who was giving him a lift and said *"I hate it when my parents go on holiday. There's no one there to talk over what you've done in a day."*

These two examples give some insight into what young people see as important. It may be that if parents knew this they might well change their behaviour and other problems might be ameliorated.

Early intervention

Early intervention is designed to create a climate in which parents and young people seek advice and support before a particular need or problem requires drastic remedies. It should also occur in circumstances where no one feels stigmatised by their use of a particular service.

The Children Act 1989, the Children (Scotland) Act 1995 and the Children (Northern Ireland) Order 1995 all place clear responsibilities on parents to care for their children. However, resources to help them carry out these responsibilities are often limited to particular services such as disability. Parents may also have problems understanding and carrying out their parenting role and training could be provided in the short-term. Parenting skills should also be part of the National Curriculum. However, Mike Jarman of Barnardo's said recently that *"Parent education can be very effective ... but only works where parents really want to learn."*

Early intervention can create a framework for the support of young people and families before they encounter difficulties, and families can gain support to deal with problems within the family rather than members having to leave the family to gain the help they need. Early intervention, by enabling young people and families to deal with problems more effectively, reduces the adverse effects these problems might have on other children and family members. It also reduces the likelihood of a spiral of, for example, bullying, substance misuse, school exclusions or anti-social activity developing and thus increasing the difficulty of intervening to meet a particular need or problem.

Early intervention should start from working **with** parents as equals throughout the processes of assessment, diagnosis and planning. Even where mothers are involved, fathers are often ignored either directly by not asking them to be involved or indirectly by making appointments and meetings when fathers are not likely to be there. This gives a feeling on the part of many fathers that they do not have any responsibilities for bringing up their family. Having failed to involve them in the initial processes, professionals are then surprised when fathers do not see themselves as having a role to play in any decisions or in carrying out those decisions.

Traditionally, early intervention has been targeted at particular groups but it is notoriously difficult to predict who will and who will not require a particular service. This is especially so when changes in people's circumstances can make them fall in and out of the proposed net. Early intervention should be seen as the first, rather than, the last problem solving tool to be used either individually by professionals or jointly with other specialists.

Research

The recent Rowntree study was based on 2800 fathers and 3192 mothers all of whom were members of the National Child Development Study. This study has regularly traced the lives of those born in Britain in one week in 1958. This latest research gives some indicators of families who may need help in the future. It also highlights areas where early intervention might prevent such need. Most of the information on which this study was based was collected when the members were aged 33. The full report *Parenting in the 1990s* by Elsa Ferri and Kate Smith is published by the Family Policy Studies Centre in association with the Joseph Rowntree Foundation.

Over 50 per cent of those in the study were categorised as 'dual earner' or 'work rich' and were generally better qualified, had higher status occupation and higher incomes. Just four per cent of the sample parents were in households with no earner but this group had four or more children. This means that a disproportionately large number of children were in the bottom quarter of income distribution.

There was little evidence to suggest an erosion of family life occurred when both parents were in full-time employment. In this context, family life means joint activities such as family meals, outings, or contact with family and friends. It is long hours, particularly when fathers work more than 50 hours per week, rather than the fact of employment itself which have a detrimental effect. The survey found:

- More than one in four fathers worked 50 hours a week or more, and those who did were less involved in family activities.

- Fathers in dual full-time earner households were more likely than those in other employment situations to share in childcare and domestic work, but their contribution was reduced considerably if they worked long hours.

- Among employed mothers, the discontent of those with partners who were uninvolved with their children increased with the number of hours they themselves worked. Four out of ten mothers working 35 hours or more a week reported that they were unhappily married and generally dissatisfied.

- By contrast, fathers marital happiness and satisfaction with life were only tenuously linked to their involvement with their children.

- Parents in single-earner families, with only the father in employment, were, marginally, the most happy with their marital relationships and the most satisfied with their lives in general.
- The dual earner household was the most common employment situation, although mothers were twice as likely to be in part-time jobs.
- The severe economic disadvantages suffered by households with no earner affects a disproportionately large number of children, as these also tended to be the largest families.
- There was little evidence of a markedly greater contribution to family life from fathers who were not in employment even when their wives were in paid work. These mothers thus appeared to carry a particularly heavy burden of employment outside the home **plus** major responsibility for domestic tasks.

There were few marked differences in the ways in which parents in different employment situations treated their children. Children with two full-time working parents were expected to make a greater contribution to their own self-care and domestic chores than those in other households.

The National Children's Bureau is currently undertaking research within local authority areas in order to ensure partnership with parents is actively promoted and to encourage greater acceptance of parental responsibility.

Parents

John Hudson's paper on *Working with Parents* notes that there are very few, if any, inherently bad parents. Most parents who find themselves unable to carry out their responsibilities are being affected by circumstances. These may include:

- lack of knowledge, experience and/or satisfactory role models
- lack of resources to feed, clothe, house, teach or support their family
- lack of opportunity through, for example, stigma or social isolation, to provide the wide range of experiences a young person needs
- long-term stress through unemployment, poor working conditions or chronic illness

- short-term stress through redundancy, bereavement or other crisis
- relationship difficulties whether at home or in wider society
- the consequences of such relationship difficulties including separation, divorce, remarriage and step-parenting
- the indirect consequences of stress and/or relationship difficulties such as alcoholism, self-abuse and mental illness.

All work with young people must recognise that parents must be consulted about the young person, unless a court specifically states otherwise. It is in deciding, and who decides, what is in the 'young person's best interest' that the difficulty arises. Working with young people and their parents separately in the hope that ultimately there will be joint sessions later is the aim, but both might feel the need:

- for practical support
- reassurance
- to learn skills
- to develop new ways of dealing with situations
- to acknowledge differences without feeling a failure
- to realise that by acknowledging this as 'normal' can go a long way to solving, or at least reducing, the differences to manageable proportions.

In the UK the average life of a marriage is now under 10 years which means that an increasing number of young people will not be living or cannot remember living, with their family of origin. The trauma for a young person of broken relationships and the development of new ones must be addressed as well as understanding the realistic expectations from these relationships.

Working with parents

Before meeting parents it must be decided:

- why a meeting is necessary
- should the young person attend in the first instance – discuss with the young person
- what it is hoped the meeting will achieve.

When meeting parents it is important to look at what the adolescent wants, what the parents want, what it is possible to achieve and then make a plan. You may think either party needs to change their way of behaving but both sets of feelings must be considered. The negotiating skills section may help here.

If you are in the parents' home it will give you an opportunity to learn about the adolescent at home which may be very different from the young person you know.

When you meet parents you must meet as equals. It should be a two-way process. You must also assume they have a long-term positive interest in their child's future – whatever the short-term evidence to the contrary might be. This may have arisen from the stress of their present situation. You may also need to encourage them to remain as involved with their young person as they feel able and as the young person will permit. They need to be involved in decision-making and kept in touch with progress even where they have no or minimal involvement with the young person.

Sometimes other family members or family friends can be used as 'go-betweens' to help get the young person back home if he or she is 'looked after'. They might also act as a mediator where communication has broken down within the family and the young person is threatening to leave home.

Sometimes you may decide to offer counselling to parents. Explain what this means and what the implications might be. Whatever happens, you cannot force the pace. You have to allow time for parents to come to you.

Family conferencing is a way of involving families in the decision making process. This was developed in New Zealand and is now finding favour in many parts of this country. Family conferencing is designed to enable families to make decisions about their children with support from professionals. A meeting is called for all interested parties which is in a suitable location and at an appropriate time for the parents and other family members. Various matters are discussed and then the professionals leave and the family make a plan for solving the particular problem. The plan is then implemented with support from the professionals.

Where

Where you meet parents will have an effect on the likelihood of a successful outcome. Many parents will have adverse memories of school so meetings in schools may cause fear or be unsettling. A student once said that the one thing her mother was looking forward to when she left school was not having to come to parents' evenings. One school, when inviting parents to informal meetings, suggests they use a side entrance which saves them having to walk through often daunting entrance halls. Social services offices do not have good connotations and children's homes where their children have been placed 'after the social worker has taken them from them!' would certainly not seem an ideal place for any form of conciliatory meeting

If you are invited to the parents' home then it is important to remember that you are the guest in their home and should behave accordingly. You should also respect their way of life.

When

Many parents work and meetings that are called during the day often mean a loss of pay or the goodwill of an employer. Meetings should be called that are convenient to all parties and if they must be during normal working hours should either be at the beginning or the end of a working day. Meetings that involve young people should be held after school.

Child care provision/interpreters should also be offered if this is appropriate for any meetings.

Why

The reason for a meeting should be explained to the parents. It may be to help, assist, ameliorate, guide, arbitrate or just support the family. *"I've just popped round to see how things are going"* may be all that is needed or may be the trigger to the family telling you about other concerns where they think you may be able to help.

Building up trust

The police know the value of visiting families to build up trust. Often they will call round to visit a family who may be called to give evidence. This moral support which families find very beneficial usually means that the police have a better chance of obtaining a conviction. It may be that other professionals could similarly visit families on an informal basis and thus show that someone cares.

What you wear

Is it important? Some would say no. However, if you wish to create the right atmosphere in order to achieve success then you need to think about the family and respect what you judge to be appropriate dress – very casual may be right for one family and equally inappropriate for another.

How you behave

Always treat the family with respect. Come on time if you have made an appointment, say how long the meeting will be, listen to what is said even if you don't agree. You don't have to accept the offer of a cup of tea if you think the standard of cleanliness leaves something to be desired!

Tell parents that anything they tell you will always be confidential. If you are going to pass on any information, always tell them. Also let them see what you have written down and give them a copy. Any suggestions you make must suit the family's way of life. Some parents may shout. You must keep calm and try to work out alternative strategies with which they are happy.

Alone or accompanied

Sometimes visiting a family alone is the best strategy. At other times for your own safety it may be better to be accompanied. If someone else is with you, one of you can talk/work with the parents and the other with the young person.

Strategy

Have a plan before the meeting and try not to allow circumstances to make you digress. Have a safety strategy – one researcher who visits families in their homes said she always carries a collapsible umbrella and a mobile 'phone! At the end of the meeting state what has been agreed, what has to be done and when contact will be made again.

Practical suggestions for working with parents

- Thank the parents for their contribution, no matter how small.
- Don't get involved or sidetracked by other events.
- Although you have a plan you may have to play 'it by ear'.
- Sometimes what you see and hear will be emotionally disturbing and take its toll on you – be prepared.
- Be focused – what you hear may be interesting but not relevant to the task you wish to successfully achieve.
- Don't be shocked by the home environment.
- The young person may not want you to meet the parents or may not want to maintain contact. Respect their wishes. Try again at a later date.
- Other members of the extended family may be the starting point.
- Be sensitive – parents may not accept, know or care whether there is anything wrong.

If you get to know parents better you may be better able to understand the young person. However, it is important not to lose sight of the fact that you are working with, and advocating for, the adolescent and that working with parents is one of many ways that it may be possible for you to help the young person.

Chapter 6

Successful communication

It is arguable that adolescents, because of their unpredictable mood swings, are the most difficult people with whom to communicate successfully.

When dealing with adolescents three things are important. The first is to be realistic in target setting, i.e. what is achievable? Failure to set realistic targets can lead to stress and loss of confidence. The second is to remember to communicate long-term rather than short-term as success today may in fact make tomorrow's communication more difficult. The third is that, given the problems in communicating successfully with adolescents, it is vital that the communicator has a clear plan or philosophy for communicating and is fully aware of the communication process and options available.

This chapter will:
1. re-visit the communication process
2. give reminders of the tools and techniques
3. discuss a philosophy for establishing the right climate for communicating
4. consider some practical techniques designed to improve the chances of success.

The communication process

Communication is about sending and receiving information. Before beginning to communicate it is worth considering the following :
- are the conditions right for good communication?
- what is the best medium for the particular communication?
- how will we judge the success or otherwise of the communication?

Let us deal with these in reverse order.

Setting success criteria

A successful communication is one where the **outcome of the communication** is the **one intended** by the sender.

Communication is about **action** and **reaction**. If the receiver of a communication **acts** the way the sender intended them to act and *feels* the way the sender wanted them to feel then the communication is successful.

It is important for long-term success to get both **action and reaction** right. Getting one right is not too difficult for example *"Go to your room – now!"* This may get the desired **action** in the short-term but what is the long-term effect?

Transactional analysis, stroking and the trading stamps analogy

Anyone who is serious about improving their communication skills will benefit from studying transactional analysis. TA simplifies and explains the psychology of the communication process.

Transactional analysis is a complex title for a subject that is otherwise simple. It was developed by a Canadian-born American psychoanalyst named Eric Berne. His theories achieved popularity with the publication of his book *The Games People Play*. They became more popular after Berne's associate, Thomas Harris published his later book, *I'm O.K., You're O.K.*

These books were aimed primarily at psychiatric and psychologically based practitioners. However, direct and pragmatic applications of transactional analysis came later following various publications by Dorothy Jongeward, Muriel James and Jut Meininver.

In order to assess the quality of your communication the trading stamp analogy as used in transactional analysis is useful. The trading stamp analogy is a simple way of assessing communications (transactions) based on the stroking principle.

Stroking

From the moment of birth every person has the need to be touched physically. A child cannot grow successfully into maturity without positive physical stroking by its mother or mother substitute. This 'stroke hunger' has been proved to be one of the greatest of human hungers. Without physical caressing, babies die or wither away.

Positive strokes

During the first few years of our lives we are continually stroked by our parents and other relatives. That is, we receive caresses and pats by people bigger than we are. Without this positive physical stroking the child cannot develop and withdraws into itself.

After about age two it is no longer culturally acceptable to stroke people physically except within the closest of relationships. Instead we begin looking for other methods of recognition. These can be non-verbal such as a wink of an eye, or a pat on the back. However, most forms of positive stroking involve verbal stimuli or responses, usually seen in the form of compliments. The need for physical stroking is sublimated into something which substitutes for it even though it is not as good.

Conditional or mixed strokes

A form of positive stroking which is not quite so good, but better than no strokes at all, is conditional. A conditional stroke is still positive; however, it has a condition attached to the positive feeling. If one gives a person a compliment in the following way it is a conditional stroke; *"If you get your room tidy by tonight, I'll let you watch TV."* These are sometimes called 'mixed strokes'.

Negative strokes

There are some parents who ignore and fail to give positive recognition to their children either verbally or physically for many reasons. Sometimes this is because in their own childhood they were themselves not touched enough, and they learned to keep their distance from other adults. This can be passed on to their children and these children often gain the habit of collecting negative strokes. It is better, it is said, to receive a reprimand rather than no recognition at all. At least one knows that one is alive and that other people are aware of it.

At the same time there are people who provide negative strokes to others having learned this method of approach as a child. Generally however people provide others with a mixture of positive and negative strokes as well as being recipients of both positive and negative strokes. People become uncomfortable if they receive or give too many or too few positive or negative strokes based upon the stroking patterns with which they grew up. This is known as their individual 'stroke balance'.

There is a mythology which states that if you provide others with too many positive strokes, you may run out of them yourself – 'there might not be enough to go around.' This is known as the 'stroke economy' and is obviously incorrect although subconsciously believed by many.

The trading stamp analogy

When we receive strokes, whether they be positive, conditional or negative, we are left with a psychological feeling. We also gain a psychological feeling if we receive no strokes at all. Positive strokes leave us with feelings of gladness, joy, warmth and good humour and some conditional strokes may serve to heighten the same feelings but not to the same degree. When we receive negative strokes, or no strokes at all, our feelings can be those of depression, anger, guilt, suspicion, frustration, boredom and other related unpleasant sensations.

We treat these feelings in two ways, either getting rid of them immediately or saving them to be expressed later in a variety of ways. Eric Berne saw a comparison with what we do with our feelings and what many people do with trading stamps, as used in some shops. In some stores when we purchase goods we are given a number of trading stamps which are issued in proportion to the amount of money we spend (these may be known as 'bonus points', 'air miles' or even 'brownie points'). These stamps were taken home, usually, and pasted into specially designed books, although some people left their stamps behind. When a certain number of books of stamps were filled, these were cashed in for a 'free' gift or prize. A few stamps gets us a small prize and lots of stamps can be cashed in for a better prize.

Berne saw that we treat our feelings in the same way. Some of us tend not to collect feelings, merely leaving them behind and moving on to the next incident in life. Most of us collect them and save them in various amounts.

We can 'redeem' these feelings in various quantities, depending upon how many we like to save in our 'collections' for 'free' emotional prizes, either small or large.

Every time a communication (transaction) takes place both parties subconsciously value the transaction. Each party to the transaction feels varying degrees of goodness or badness about the transaction. Depending on the rating, they **subconsciously** put stamps into the imaginary book – black for a bad transaction, gold for a good transaction. The amount of stamps is in proportion to the goodness or badness of the transaction. This is true of every transaction even the most simple such as saying *'hello'*. The stamps can be allowed to mount up, or they may be cashed in at any time. For example, some people have a relationship based on swapping insults in a friendly way. One jibe or sarcastic comment is met by another. Here the books are stamped then cashed in on a regular basis. A similar relationship can exist based on good stamps where simple compliments or flattery – *"I like your suit"* are met with a suitable response – *"Thanks, I think your shoes are nice"*.

In other relationships the stamps accrue and are only cashed in when a considerable amount have been collected. Consider an older girl who has consistently bullied a younger boy for many weeks or months. The boy will have been subconsciously stamping the black book all this time. Eventually a situation will arise when the boy will be in a position to get his own back and make things really bad for the girl, thus cashing in the large amount of stamps. Equally, in a situation where a resident has been particularly good to a carer over a long period, the carer will have accrued a large collection of gold stamps in the imaginary book and is likely to cash in the stamps by doing something that in the normal course of events would be classed as **'beyond the call of duty'**.

The trading stamps analogy is extremely useful for gauging the success or otherwise of any communication. All you need to do is pause during or after the communication and ask yourself – *"If I was stamping a book at the moment – what colour stamps and how many would I be putting in the book"*. You can usually bet that if you are putting in black stamps, so is the other person.

The trading stamp analogy is a great help in ensuring that you do not just communicate in the short-term. For example, if you can get angry with someone and browbeat them into doing something such as *'tidy your room immediately'*, you have communicated successfully in the short-term, but unsuccessfully in the long-term – plenty of black stamps being collected!

Very large lifetime collections of black stamps can be traded in for equally large 'free prizes' such as heart attacks, suicides or divorces.

If in your communication you can avoid too many black stamp situations then you will avoid arousing defensive behaviour in the young people with whom you work. Much of the behaviour that young people exhibit is **caused** by their perception of the motives and attitudes of the adults who are trying to help them.

Avoiding defensive behaviour

We communicate with adolescents to state objectives, praise good behaviour, introduce new systems, counsel them, decide on courses of action and so on. Difficulties can arise when doing this if the adult, despite being well-intentioned, arouses defensive reactions.

We should remember that communication is a **people** process rather than a **language** process and all communication provokes action of some sort. In other words it motivates. If you wish to improve your communication, you should look carefully at your inter-personal relationships. In particular, ensure that you reduce the chance of causing defensive behaviour.

What sort of communication causes defensive behaviour and how can it be avoided?

Defensive behaviour occurs when an individual perceives **threats** or anticipates threats in the group. Young people who behave defensively, whilst giving some attention to the group task, devote much energy to self-defence. Besides attending to the task, they think more about how they appear to others, how to be seen more favourably, how to win, dominate, impress or escape punishment, and/or how to avoid or mitigate a perceived or anticipated threat.

The young person's own inner feelings will in turn affect actions and these actions will tend to create similar defensive postures in others. If unchecked, the ensuing response becomes increasingly defensive. In short, defensive behaviour causes defensive listening. This in turn produces facial, postural and verbal cues which raise the defence level of the original communicator. Once defensive behaviour is aroused in a listener, she or he can no longer listen properly; cannot concentrate on the message that is being sent – concentrating instead on other messages which it is believed are being sent.

Defensive communicators send off multiple value, motive and effect cues. Also defensive recipients distort what they receive. As a person becomes more and more defensive, they become less and less able to understand the motives, the values and the emotions of the sender. Defensive behaviour can be avoided if the sender ensures that a supportive or defense reductive climate is maintained.

If the sender is successful in maintaining a supportive climate, the receiver will read less into the communication and will accept it for what it is. As defensive behaviour reduces, so the receiver is better able to concentrate on the structure, the content, and the meaning of the message.

Six pairs of defensive and supportive categories of communication:

Defensive	*Supportive*
Evaluation	Descriptive
Control	Problem orientation
Strategy	Spontaneity
Neutrality	Empathy
Superiority	Equality
Closed mind	Open mind

Any behaviour which the receiver perceives as possessing any of the characteristics in the left-hand column will arouse defensiveness, whereas that which the receiver interprets as having characteristics designated as supportive, reduces defensive feelings. The degree to which the reactions occur (how many black or gold stamps) depends upon the personal level of defensiveness and upon the general climate in the group at the time.

Evaluation and description

Speech or other behaviour that appears to the receiver as evaluative increases defensiveness. If by expression, posture, manner of speech, tone of voice or the words used, the sender appears to be evaluating or judging the receiver, then the receiver goes on guard. However, other factors may lessen the reactions. If the listener thinks that the sender regards them as an equal and is being open and spontaneous, for example, the evaluativeness in the message will be neutralised and perhaps not even perceived. The same principle applies equally to the other five categories of potentially defence-producing climates as the six sets are interactive.

Adults' attitudes towards young people are frequently, of necessity, evaluative. It is difficult, however, to frame expressions that will not appear judgmental to a defensive person.

The simple question *"Who did that?"* is more often than not received as an accusation. This is not surprising as speech is so often judgmental and there is good reason for the defensive reactions that are so common. An insecure person, whether in a group or a one-to-one situation, is likely to place blame, to see others as either good or bad, to make moral judgments of others, and to question the value and motives of the speech they hear.

Descriptive speech, in contrast to that which is evaluative, tends to arouse a minimum of suspicion and uneasiness. Speech which the listener **sees** as a genuine request for information, or as material with neutral loadings is descriptive. Examples are – the presentation of feelings, events, perceptions, or processes which do not ask or imply that the listener changes his or her behaviour or attitude. It is very difficult to avoid overtone when doing this as is illustrated by news items reporting on such matters as political parties or religious groups.

How can we use this in practical situations? The question *"Who moved that chair?"* is likely to get an answer such as *"Search me, I've been working all morning"*, or, *"Chair – which chair?"* A statement such as *"I see the chair had to be moved"* may get the reply *"Yes, it was in the way where it was so I moved it this morning"*.

Control and problem orientation

Speech and other behaviour which is used to control evokes resistance. Most of our communication is about trying to change an attitude, or to influence behaviour. The more open the effort to control is, the less defensive the receiver will become. Any suspicion that the attempt to control is being hidden will only increase the resistance. There are so many persuasive messages being aimed at people these days, on television, in politics, advertising, religion and from government, that a cynical and almost paranoid response has developed in listeners.

Implicit in all attempts to alter another person is the assumption by the sender that the person to be altered is inadequate. Once the listener believes that the sender views them as ignorant, unable to make decisions, uninformed, immature, unwise, or possessed of wrong or inadequate attitudes, he or she has a valid motive for reacting defensively.

Methods of control are many and varied. Legalistic insistence on detail, form filling, regulations and policies, conformity norms and all laws are among the methods. Gestures, facial expressions, other forms of non-verbal communication and even such simple acts as holding a door open in a particular manner are means of imposing one's will upon another and hence are potential sources of resistance.

Problem orientation on the other hand, need not arouse defensive reactions. When the sender communicates a desire to collaborate in defining a mutual problem and in seeking its solution the sender tends to create the same problem orientation in the listener. Of greater importance, the sender also implies that they have no pre-determined solution, attitude, or method to impose. By adopting this approach the sender allows the receiver to set his or her own goals, reach conclusions, make decisions and evaluate progress or to involve the sender in so doing.

It is this principle that can form the basis for a person to person contract in as much as the young person helps set their own targets for a period, rather than having them set for them and then at appraisal time the discussion of performance relative to the targets can be conducted in an atmosphere of problem orientation rather than control.

Strategy and spontaneity

When the sender is thought to be 'scheming', the receiver becomes defensive. The attention is then on solving the question *"What is the sender up to?"* rather than on listening to the real message. No one wishes to be a guinea pig, a role player and no one likes to be duped.

If the listener thinks that a strategy is being used to hide the true motive they will tend to enlarge whatever they think is being concealed, and the amount of defensiveness will increase accordingly (black stamps). It is not only in the sender that strategic behaviour can exist or be thought to exist. Sometimes the receiver can, by nods of agreement, posture, facial expressions and other forms of behaviour, cause the sender to believe that the message is not being taken seriously. If this happens the sender may stop communicating, believing that 'a listening technique' is being used. The strongest reactions usually come when a person believes that a strategy is being made to look spontaneous.

For example, a person who regularly says *"Oh dear, look at the time. I must go to a meeting"* would incur much less resentment by just excusing themselves honestly.

Similarly, people who pretend to be simple souls when they are clearly not so arouse defensiveness in others. This strong aversion to deceit can explain the general resistance to politicians who are suspected of behind-the-scenes planning to get votes, or to the sophisticated, smooth, or clever person whose 'spin doctoring' is not trusted.

Conversely, behaviour that appears to be spontaneous and free from deception is defense reductive. If the communicator is seen as having uncomplicated motives, as being straightforward and honest, and as behaving spontaneously in response to the situation, he or she is likely to **cause** a positive response (gold stamps).

Neutrality and empathy

When neutrality in speech or behaviour appears to the receiver to indicate a lack of concern for their welfare, people become defensive. Young people like to be thought of as valuable people, as individuals of special worth, of concern and affection. The clinical, detached attitude on the part of many psychologists, doctors, and other professionals is resented by young people. Detached speech which communicates little warmth or caring is in such contrast to the effect laden speech in social situations that it often communicates rejection.

Communication which conveys empathy for the feelings and respect for the worth of the listener, however, reduces defensiveness. When the speaker communicates that he or she identifies with the listener's problems, acknowledges, but not necessarily agrees with, their feelings, and accepts the emotional reactions at face value, the listener is reassured.

The combination of understanding and empathising with the other person's emotions with no accompanying attempt to change the person is highly supportive. Also spontaneous facial and bodily gestures showing concern are usually interpreted as especially valid evidence of deep level concern.

Superiority and equality

When a person communicates to another that they feel superior in position, power, wealth, intellectual ability, physical characteristics, or other ways, they arouse defensiveness.

The listener, because of feelings of inadequacy, interprets the message in a negative way looking for the effects of the message rather than the true message. The listener reacts by not hearing the message, by forgetting it, by competing with the sender or by becoming jealous. If the listener thinks the sender believes themself to be superior it is taken as an indication that the sender is not willing to enter into a shared problem solving relationship, that feedback is not required, that help is not needed and/or that they will be likely to try to reduce the power, the status and the worth of the receiver.

Many ways exist for creating the atmosphere that the sender feels equal to the listener. Defensive behaviour is reduced when the sender is seen to be willing to enter into participative planning with mutual trust and respect. Differences in talent, ability, worth, appearance, status and power must be minimised if defensive behaviour in the listener is to be avoided.

Open mind and closed mind

People who know all the answers, need no additional data and who regard themselves as teachers rather than co-workers, tend to put others on guard. What is more, people who make dogmatic statements are often thought of by the listener as someone covering up inward feelings of uncertainty. Dogmatic people are seen as needing to be right and wanting to win an argument rather than solve a problem. Dogmatic behaviour is often considered as an attempt to control.

Defensive behaviour in the listener can be avoided when the sender indicates that he or she is willing to modify their own behaviour, attitudes and ideas. The person who appears to be **investigating** issues rather than taking sides, to be problem solving rather than debating, and who is willing to explore new ideas tends to communicate that the listener may have something of value to contribute. A person who is genuinely looking for information does not resent help.

What follows are some practical tips that will help to put the above theory into practice.

Communication — tools and methods

Communication is about sending and receiving information. This can be done in many ways. The following chart shows the various ways of sending and receiving information.

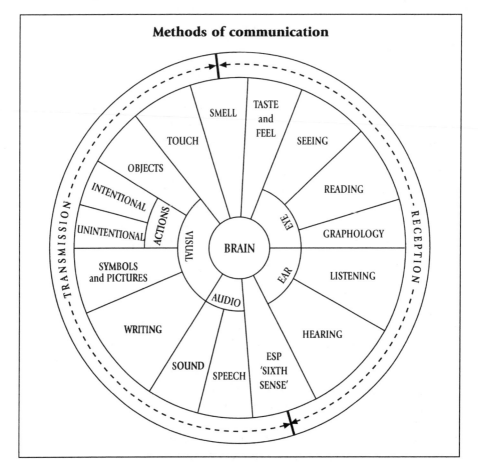

The toolkit

Let us consider each of the tools:

Touch
Touch is the most powerful of all communication tools. Touch is the bottom line of communication. Think of a person and decide in what circumstances you would touch that person. In what way would you touch them. Where on their body would you touch them; for how long would you touch them? When you have the answers to these questions you will know exactly what your relationship is with that person. Because touch is so powerful, it can work well for you if judged correctly. However, because it is so powerful it can seriously damage your relationship with anyone if you get it wrong.

If you are **certain** that it is appropriate to, say, put your arm around someone to comfort them, or reinforce a point then do it. In some cases it devalues your communication if you do not do it. However, you must be **certain** that it is appropriate – get it wrong and you collect many black stamps. If in doubt, limit your touching to conventional touching, i.e. shaking hands on greeting and on departure – but do it!

Objects
Often they can convey understanding better than words. How would you describe a corkscrew and how it works to someone who has not encountered one before? Most practical things such as repairing a puncture or making a cake are better communicated by showing rather than by telling.

Actions, intentional
Some actions help communication and should be intentionally used. In other words, done as routine, not left to chance. An obvious example is the one mentioned earlier, i.e. shaking hands on meeting or leaving a person.

There are many other actions that can aid your communication such as being deliberately formal or informal. You can deliberately dress and behave formally or informally in order to influence a communication. For example if you want to elicit information from a person it is better to do so in a comfortable way, i.e. in informal settings such as in a café, in your home, in a place where you can sit side by side or at a slight angle, perhaps have a cup of tea or coffee, wear casual clothes and generally convey a relaxed message. Equally, if you have some serious points to make such as a result of indiscipline then this is better done formally, across a desk or table, sat in upright chairs, dressed formally. All these convey the seriousness of the business at hand. Written communications usually convey formality, unless it is just a note written on a scrap of paper, so if you want to impress on a person that you are serious about something – a meeting or a complaint, then take notes and/or confirm it in writing.

Intentionally putting yourself on the same level as the other person will aid the communication process. If they are sitting – you sit. If they are standing you stand.

Shaking hands is a good way of making clear to someone that the conversation is over, whilst reinforcing the fact that your relationship is still OK. A typical case might be a disciplinary or change type of interview where you want to end it clearly and positively and you might say *"OK John, we're agreed then that in future you will be in before midnight and that I will not wait up for you. Let's give it a go"* and at this point you offer to shake hands, cementing the deal and ending the conversation.

Actions, unintentional
These are things that we do without being aware that we do them such as stabbing a finger at someone in order to emphasise a point. There may also be things we do that we cannot prevent ourselves doing such as blushing.

Unintentional actions do cause communication problems and it is wise to be watchful and critical of your behaviour in order to try to eliminate some of the inadvertent/unintentional actions that might be harming your communication. Often when we communicate we start to feel bad about something but decide not to show our feelings – a mistake. Our body language will give the game away. Such things as frowning, eyes narrowing, fidgeting, clenched fists, tightening of the jaw resulting in a change of voice pitch, all these are give-aways. Much better to come clean and say something like *"what you are telling me is making me feel ...."*

Touching people to emphasise a point, where the touching is unwelcome or inappropriate will not only send bad vibes to the recipient, it will prevent them from concentrating on the point you are making.

Invading people's space, getting too close to them, is another unintentional action of which many people are guilty. In some cases it is a deliberate/intentional action, i.e. trying to create an atmosphere of friendliness or conspiracy. This is a bad feeling because it is unwelcome.

The clothes you wear can turn people on or off. Obviously your dress is your own business and you have the right to choose. However, you should bear in mind that it might be hindering your ability to communicate. Over or under-dressing for the occasion or the audience is a common problem. The following are two examples:

- A teenage girl went for an interview for a part-time job at her local supermarket. She wore her best clothes, the ones she wore when going out in the evening which included a fairly low cut blouse and a pair of very high heeled shoes. The interviewer decided that if she judged incorrectly what to wear for interview it was likely she would not be able to judge the best ways of handling customers. She did not get the job.

- A male teacher in his fifties joined the school and on his first day he was wearing very casual fashion clothes, almost identical to those worn by his students. The students laughed at him and could not respect him.

The point here is not to suggest that you might dress or behave in a calculated way, but to remind you that in certain circumstances you might be well advised to consider some changes. You have to decide on priorities. *"Is success with the adolescent my top priority, or is my right to dress and act as I wish my top priority?"*

Symbols and pictures

A picture or symbol is worth a thousand words. Do not be afraid to draw or sketch out an idea, it may help to get the message across. Signs often get a message across in a softer way than words. For example which do you prefer to see?

NO SMOKING or

Writing

This is an over-rated form of communication, although in many circumstances it is still the best tool we have. The things that prevent the written word from being successful are:

- you cannot ask it questions
- it is too long and complicated
- you do not know what the words mean
- you cannot convey the 'feel' of the message
- the receiver has difficulty with reading.

If you must use the written word to confirm or make a communication, bear in mind the following advice:

- use short simple words and not long complicated ones
- use short sentences and vary the length of the sentences. A range of 5-30 words for sentences with an average sentence length of 17 words is recommended.
- before you send it, get someone else to read it and tell you if they think it is clear
- ask the recipient what they think of the written things you send them.

Sounds

These can affect people positively or negatively. Lively music is played at rail terminals early in the day to get people to move briskly. In the evening gentle music is played to calm frayed tempers at the end of a long working day and so reduce the chances of conflict.

The music played in many high street stores annoys older people – but too many stores play this music for it to be coincidence – you can be sure that there is evidence that it influences young people to buy the products. You might like to consider whether or not some background music might be appropriate for some of the discussions that you have with the young people.

Speech

The most common communication tool is speech. However, problems might occur as a result of:

- poor pronunciation or dialect
- speaking too fast or too slow

- poor choice of words
- words having different meanings in different places and for different generations
- trying to be 'with it' by using teenage words. This will not help (black stamps).

To improve your chances of success – use simple words and speak clearly and as slowly as is comfortable. If you naturally speak quickly then do not artificially slow down as this will inhibit you – however if you leave bigger gaps between each sentence this will help to give the listener a better chance of grasping the message.

When communicating using speech – remember the 80-20 rule.

If you do **20%** of the **speaking** and **80%** of the **listening** you stand a good chance of hearing something useful and you will in all probability earn a few gold stamps.

Listening

The best listeners are the best communicators

Listening is not a passive process – it is an active process.

Active listening is a combination of using the ears and eyes to receive messages and signals, backed up by actions such as nodding and verbal prompting which show the speaker that you are interested and that you are taking notice of what is being said.

It is not enough to listen with your ears. You must **show** that you are listening. You must be active. You must expend some energy. Being active can include:

- nodding
- taking notes
- occasionally interrupting to check on a point
- interjections such as: *'Really' 'Gosh!' 'Wow!'*
- asking questions.

The best listeners know what questions to ask and when to use them. Four key types of question are the:

- open question
- closed question
- mirror question and
- probe.

How do these work and when should we use them?

Open questions

These are the ones to use to get someone started – they often start with *"Tell me about ... your work, your school, your family ...."* They do not require a specific answer and the questioner has no idea where the answer may lead.

The question *"Tell me about your school?"* may get a response beginning *"It was a comprehensive, boys only ..."* or *" It was a tall grey building, set back in trees ..."* or *"I hated it and everything about it ..."*. Open questions are for getting people started and for finding out about people. They work because mostly they are perceived to be non-threatening. Plenty of open questions at the start of a conversation will give you a good idea of the likes, dislikes and attitudes of the person you are with.

Closed questions

Open questions are not good for finding out **specific** information – you need closed questions for this. Closed questions require a specific answer like *'Yes'*, *'No'*, *'One Hundred'*, *'Yesterday'*, *'Three o'clock'*. When you need to get at the facts, or to pin someone down, or to stop them waffling a closed question is what you need. Closed questions can be threatening – which is why it is unwise to use them too early in a conversation as this can cause defensiveness.

Many TV chat show hosts enjoy an undeserved reputation as good interviewers. Usually the guest is only too ready to chat – so any old question will do – usually a closed question. *"You've just written a book haven't you?"* (closed). *"As a matter of fact I have ... blah blah blah ... "* He or she then talks about the book for five minutes – as planned. Watch the same interviewer with a taciturn guest. *"So you are over here to promote your new film?"* *"Yes."* *"The opening is tomorrow isn't it?"* *"Yes."* *"And you're co-starring with X aren't you?" "I am."* Imagine the answer to a question such as *"Tell me about your new film?"*

Be aware of the type of question that you use. If you do not seem to be good at getting information from people it may be that you are using the wrong questions (closed instead of open). If you want to get a conversation back on track or to stop a waffler or to change the subject – interrupt with a closed question – *"Excuse me – how many did you say there were?" "OK– so when exactly was that?" "Did you say there were three of them?"*

When the person stops to answer the question you can gain the initiative, sometimes called 'getting the ball back' and step in with a supplementary question that will take the conversation in the required direction – *"OK – so there were three of them and Bill was one of them. Now tell me about ..."* This technique is not foolproof but it will work nine times out of ten.

Two other questioning techniques make up a very useful quartet. These are the mirror and the probe.

The mirror
This is as simple as it sounds. All you do is repeat what the speaker has just said in order to show that you are listening. *"School – I really hated it!" "You really hated it?" "Yes – The teachers were horrid!" "The teachers were horrid?"* Obviously this must not be overdone but it is an excellent way of showing that you are listening and prompting the person to continue.

The probe
The probe is used when you are not sure that you have fully understood the message or when you think the message may be incomplete. Probes are similar to closed questions in that they seek clarification – but they are also partially open in that you are not inviting a specific answer. Examples of probes are – *"So, am I right in thinking ..." "Does that mean that ..." "Let me check that I've got this right. What you're saying is ..." "So how did you feel about that?"*

Getting the conditions right

To be a successful communicator you need to feel confident – but not overconfident in your abilities. It is important that you have the confidence to say what you want to say in a non-aggressive way and at the same time be open to opposing views and arguments knowing that you can recognise them and discuss them without having to agree with them or give in to them. This is called being assertive. Being assertive means that you can:

Persist
You can, if necessary, say what you want, over and over again – like a faulty CD player. Calm repetition is often more effective than rehearsed arguments or the expression of angry feelings. Tactful persistence allows you to feel comfortable by ignoring manipulative traps, argumentative baiting and irrelevant logic, while sticking to your point.

Accept
You can accept manipulative criticism, by calmly acknowledging the probability **that there may be** some truth in what your critic says. This approach then allows you to judge for yourself what, if anything, you want to do about it. You can receive criticism comfortably, without becoming anxious or defensive, while giving no reward to manipulative or malicious criticism.

Recognise
Simple clues in a conversation indicate what is interesting or important to a young person. Recognising these clues allow you to feel less shy in entering into a conversation while prompting others to talk about themselves.

Agree
You can accept your errors and faults, without having to apologise, by agreeing with criticism of your negative qualities. This allows you to look **more** comfortably at your 'negatives', without feeling defensive and anxious. This is easier than denying or trying to hide weaknesses and it reduces your critic's anger or hostility.

Ask
You can actively ask for criticism with the idea of using the information if helpful, or exhausting it, if manipulative, while promoting the critic to be more assertive and less dependent on manipulative ploys. This allows you to seek criticism in close relationships, while getting the other to express honest negative feelings and so improve communication.

Disclose

You can initiate and accept discussion on the positive and negative aspects of your behaviour, lifestyle and intelligence to enhance communication and reduce manipulation. This allows you to disclose relevant aspects of yourself and your life that previously caused feelings of ignorance or anxiety.

Contributing at meetings

You may have to attend a meeting with or on behalf of a young person. Meetings can be very stressful. It can be daunting to be in a large group or to be facing people who are in a position of authority.

Here are some suggestions that might help make the situation less stressful:

- Be clear on which issues you wish to be assertive and restrict your contribution to these, rather than taking a stand on every issue.
- Speak early to establish yourself as an active participant.
- When making your contribution, keep it short.
- Avoid interrupting others and do not allow others to interrupt you.
- Be aware of your non-verbal messages and keep these as assertive as possible for example, sit up, lean forward, take notes, do not doodle, dress appropriately, look at people but do not stare.
- Whenever possible get a reaction to your contributions. Ask members what they think about your ideas and statements.
- If new information leads you to change your mind, be open and honest about it, but do not apologise.
- Do not let the views of one or two influential members affect your thoughts. Raise your doubts and ask for the view of others.

When setting up a review meeting, or any other meeting for that matter, the following should be considered:

Presenting your case

Before the meeting:
Be clear:

- WHY you are doing it

- WHAT you are going to do
- WHO will be listening
- WHERE other people's contributions are needed – have they been briefed?

During the meeting:

- Announce what you are going to talk about and why, unless the chairperson has already done this.
- State your plan with the main headings only. The meeting now knows the ground you will cover and members should let you go ahead without interruption.
- Announce sub-headings at the beginning of the main heading concerned only when there are three or more.
- Make it clear when you have finished one main heading and are moving on to the next. This ensures that the meeting concentrates on one thing at a time to understand your argument.
- End by giving the meeting something specific and positive to do. To end by saying *"I hope that covers everything"* is weak and negative. Instead, *"I have explained what happened; and suggested three things that can be done. I believe the best thing to do immediately is ... Have I your agreement to go ahead?"* This concentrates their thinking and is a strong ending.

After the meeting

To ensure you get the best possible results from your presentation, you should:

- See the chairperson and check any further steps to be taken.
- See the person taking the minutes/notes of the meeting to see whether any clarification is needed.
- See the members most directly concerned, particularly those who may have expressed doubts about your recommendations, or be involved in agreed action.
- Analyse your own performance.
- Take action immediately on what has been approved, and be prepared for a possible report-back presentation meeting.

There is a list of young people's rights at reviews and other meetings on p.158. These also apply to most meetings with any young person.

If the meeting you are attending is for negotiation the following may be helpful:

- **Preparation.** Assemble the facts, be clear about the issues, consider the arguments yours/others, define objectives – yours/others, be realistic, prepare alternatives.

- **Conduct.** Have one spokesperson, know the terms of reference, receive and answer information calmly, listen to the arguments, record agreement as it occurs, keep to the point, avoid raising dead issues.

- **Define settlement.** Set it out clearly, confirm acceptance, record details of settlement and implementation plans if appropriate.

Thinking precedes communicating

"Clear thinking precedes clear communication and effective action."

The best communicators spend time preparing **before** they attempt to communicate. Clearly it is not possible to anticipate every twist and turn that a conversation or meeting might take – some **thinking** in advance is always a good idea. The object here is to clarify in your own mind the facts and inferences in any given situation. One important aspect of personal effectiveness is the ability to detect a real fact from all other facts. Reports containing apparent facts, assumed facts and reported facts are not concerned with facts at all. The need is for intellectual curiosity and persistence to ensure that what you think is an unshakeable fact really is one.

Unshakeable facts help unshakeable people to make the right decisions. Real facts are reached only by objective analysis, probing and hard work – basics that are sometimes overlooked in days of ever more sophisticated theories. It is vital to distinguish between a fact, an inference and a value judgement. To avoid confusion remember that:

A **fact** is something that we have observed ourselves with any or all of our senses. When we make a statement about it, we report what we have observed. We can say *"I saw or heard it, myself"*. All factual statements relate to the past, never the future – although facts may be expressed in the present tense.

An **inference** is a statement of what is likely, or a guess about something not available to our senses. It is a conclusion drawn from past experience on the assumption that what has happened before will happen again. We can say *"I am guessing on the basis of what I saw or heard myself"*. It is a statement about the unknown, based on the known. An inference can be related to the past, present or future.

A **judgement** is a statement of our approval or disapproval of events. Often a dangerous assumption hidden in it is that our standard or judgement is the only true one. We can say: *"I am judging it on the basis of my own standards"*.

What to do
- whenever possible, delay reactions to check assumptions
- act on the calculated risk of being wrong, rather than the certainty of being right
- beware of self-fulfilling prophecy when predicting how people will behave or react.

There is no infallible method of thinking straight or indeed of getting the right answer, but a methodical approach is better than a 'hit and miss' intuitive approach.

Have logical steps of reasoning:
- **Recognise** what you know already, what you do not know and what you need to **know** about the situation. Get the information you need and take advice if appropriate. Organise your facts and classify them into a usable form.
- **Consider** what the young person knows, does not know and needs to know about the situation, then:
- **Decide** what is relevant/irrelevant for your purpose.
- **Evaluate all possible courses of action**, including doing nothing, with their pros and cons i.e. everything that **can be done**, as distinct from **ought to be** done.

Then, and only then decide on your course of action and how to implement it.

Getting the climate right/setting the rules of engagement – before attempting to communicate on specifics it is advisable to agree on an overall working arrangement – rules of engagement might be a better term. We can learn from other disciplines. In TQM (Total Quality Management) people are advised to agree individual contracts between themselves and their work colleagues. This easily understood principle could be applied to relationships.

The principle is best described by Crosby, a TQM guru using his 3 plate analogy as developed from the BBC Training Notes *Crosby on Quality.*

Crosby's 3 plate analogy

Imagine the adolescent is the middle plate. The adult is both the supplier and customer.

As a **supplier** you will supply information or a service or a product – something tangible – to the adolescent. You can talk to the adolescent and agree what the requirements are. Remember – it is OK to say no if the requirements are not suitable.

You are also the **customer** of the adolescent and you require certain information/services or product from him or her. Again you can discuss and agree this with the young person.

Having discussed both the 'supplier' and 'customer' requirements the next stage is to write them down and each take a copy. This is your agreed contract. It forms the basis for the way in which you will interact. It can contain anything you like but typical items might be:

- how you will and will not address each other
- how you will manage disagreements
- where and when you will meet
- what are the no-go areas or topics
- when you will review the contract.

The list could be endless but it is best to confine it to the 10 or 12 (20 maximum) **do's** that will govern your working relationship – **don'ts** are allowed but do's are better.

Remember – part of having a contract is that it is **reviewed on a regular basis** and modified when appropriate.

When used in industry, this system has proved highly successful as it ensures that both parties know what is important to the other and both know the state of play at any time.

Many people will skip a chapter in a book on communication or will not listen if they are on a communication training course. They believe that they are already good communicators. Sadly, in reality, those who believe they are good are in fact those who need the most help, advice and practice.

Chapter 7

Care and control –
Encouraging positive behaviour

The U.N. Convention on the Rights of the Child states that a young person should be enabled to live an independent life in society. Independence is important because it means we can care for ourselves – we can take decisions which ensure that we continue to grow and develop as people throughout our lives. Being part of society is important because people care about us; if no one in a society cares about us, we are no longer part of that society.

Caring for and caring about are opposite sides of the same coin. Being able to care for ourselves gives us self-respect; being cared about by others shows that others value us. We must be able to care for others and care about ourselves. If any of these is missing from our lives, we and our capacity to live an independent life in society will be diminished.

Caring about someone arises from respect for them as a person and, if we get to know them as a person usually develops into valuing them as people. We can care about a young person-without ever caring for them. If we do not care about them, our caring for them becomes routine and perfunctory, so that they do not receive the type of care that enables them to become independent. It may even become obsessive and smothering, so that the young person does not have the space to learn how to become a member of society.

There are many elements to caring for young people that will enable them to achieve success in their lives – the physical environment needs to facilitate the physical, emotional, intellectual, social, cultural and spiritual needs of the young person; the emotional and social ethos needs to encourage the development of trust and the development of relationships. Their lives also need reliability, involvement and commitment. They need to feel safe, to trust people and to learn to make relationships.

Creating an environment which extends young people's development entails adults providing a range of experiences, including opportunities to act individually and in groups, to lead and to follow, and to take risks. Giving responsibilities and setting expectations which enhance a young person's sense of self-worth are likely to reassure a young person that they are cared about and enhance their abilities to live an independent life in society. It is also important that young people have fun.

Young people who have not had an opportunity to experience satisfactory adult-young person or young person-young person relationships are likely to lack both skills in relationships and self-esteem. The former directly affects their ability to communicate with others; the latter will tend to make them passive or aggressive communicators, signs which are often seen as difficult behaviour and may lead to a spiral of increasingly difficult behaviour. Much difficult behaviour is related to boredom or stress. Boredom is often linked to daily living and stress to relationships; responses which prolong the boredom like cancelling an activity, increases the stress. Imposing sanctions or providing psychological pay offs, such as increased attention for a young person who is being difficult, are all likely to increase the poor behaviour.

Much has been written in recent years about Crisis Intervention, Anger Management, Handling Aggression and Coping with Violence. The aim of this part of the chapter is to offer positive tools and approaches which will prevent the need for these other strategies being adopted. However, it is not to say that sanctions in response to unacceptable behaviour should never be used; indeed, in certain circumstances sanctions have their place, but the strategies proposed here are to encourage positive behaviour.

Behaviour management based solely or predominately on punishing unacceptable behaviour may have long-term side effects such as:

- heightened emotional response – an emotionally charged response is likely to escalate conflict
- short term solutions – punishment might have a short term effect in improving behaviour but it does not teach more appropriate behaviour or the skills needed to better deal with the situation next time

- increase of guilt/anxiety on both sides, adult and young person
- decrease of self-esteem/feelings of being a bad person, encouraging young people to live up to the reputation
- modelling of responses if physically threatening punishment is used the young person may learn to copy the behaviour of the adult.

In general, punishments do not enhance the personal, social or emotional development of young people. Instead young people need to learn more effective choices which may include regaining self-control.

Some very brief guidelines for managing difficult behaviour are shown below; they were produced by Caring for Children. These are followed by a summary of other theories, both old and new.

There is the La Vigna model, consisting of four components – environment change, teaching new skills, reinforcement and reactive strategies – which is a method of focusing on the situation and developing change.

The well-known ABC analysis has been extended to ABCDE by David Leadbetter and Robin Trewartha in *Handling Aggression and Violence at Work*, Russell House Publishing, and this has been developed here as a coping strategy when planning an intervention.

John Treliotis from Edinburgh University and Ruth Sinclair, Director of Research at the National Children's Bureau have also carried out research into adolescence and a brief summary of their work is included. ·

Obviously, many of the theories overlap. Not all strategies work for everyone or all the time. What is important is that the knowledge is in place which leads to confidence when handling difficult situations.

Managing difficult behaviour (Caring for Children 1997)

Where adults face difficult behaviour, they need to avoid one-off responses which can lead to inconsistencies and think about how they can manage the situation. They need, at very least to consider:

- changing the situation
- understanding the meaning of the behaviour

- understanding why they find it difficult
- applying specific techniques to a particular situation
- reflecting on the behaviour and the ways they have responded to it.

Most behaviour is situational and most difficult behaviour can be influenced simply by changing the situation. For example sitting down, standing up, lowering the tone of voice, walking away or walking towards; getting someone to leave the situation or someone else to join it. The only guidelines are that the change should lower the emotional tone of the situation and decrease any perceived threat to the person displaying the difficult behaviour.

If you want to understand why the young person is being difficult, you need to engage with the young person, and possibly others in the situation, to understand the meaning of the situation. Very little difficult behaviour is mindless and young people often choose to exhibit difficult behaviour only in the presence of adults whom they trust to be able to cope with the behaviour. Thus some adults may find themselves dealing with difficult behaviour which would not have been displayed in another situation because there was no reliable adult present to witness such feelings.

Sometimes the meaning of the situation is affected by gender or race – the boy who will not give in to a man; or the girl who has strong feelings about a woman; the black young person or adult who has strong views about a white person or about someone from another ethnic group.

Another time the young person's behaviour may only be difficult to a particular adult whose expectations of behaviour are based on a different era or culture; perhaps the behaviour reminds the adult of something painful. Perhaps the adult prides themself on being able to manage particular situations and feels they will lose face either personally or among others if they do not respond to what others regard as fairly normal behaviour.

Sometimes a young person will deliberately wrong-foot an adult by their difficult behaviour; for example, where a young person has agreed to manage their own behaviour but has difficulties in so doing. The young person may present difficult behaviour to entice an adult to intervene when the appropriate response would have been to withdraw and leave the young person to take full responsibility for their behaviour.

Once you understand the meaning of the behaviour and are clear that you are not responding solely because of your own hang-ups or being drawn into controlling a young person where it is their responsibility to control themselves, it becomes possible to apply specific techniques to a particular situation.

In general, successful techniques redefine the relationship the young person should have with others whilst not rewarding the difficult behaviour. Towering over the young person or pushing them literally or metaphorically into a corner is more likely to encourage the young person to become passive or aggressive. They may then continue with the difficult behaviour. Whilst giving into them without ever trying to understand the reason for the difficult behaviour will encourage less respect for the adult and place less value on the relationship.

All successful techniques, even the simplest, reassure the young person that they are still valued; that the relationships they value will continue. It may be a familiar look, a word, a touch which, if it comes from a valued adult, may defuse an entire situation.

With a secure relationship the adult can convey surprise or expectation – *"I wouldn't have expected you to behave this way"* said quietly and confidently, may be enough to halt the behaviour.

Alternatively the adult can engage in 'planned ignoring', thus denying the young person the fuel of attention and/or confrontation which may prolong the difficult behaviour. Where gender or race affect the situation, changing the gender or race of the person dealing with the situation may have a positive effect. If that cannot be done, simply acknowledging to the young person that this may be a factor in the situation may be enough to change things.

Where the situation involves a group, it may be possible to create new groups, by suggesting that some members depart to undertake a different activity, or restructure, by suggesting that the whole group does something different.

Whatever technique is used to bring the difficult behaviour to an end, it is important that all involved have an opportunity to reflect on the behaviour and the way it was managed. The purpose of this reflection for both adults and young people is to understand how the situation arose, what its consequences were for all those involved and what strategies each might employ to avoid a repetition.

When everything fails adults often panic when it appears that their normal ways of handling difficult behaviour are likely to fail. No one can succeed every time and those who believe they, or anyone else can, are deluding themselves. Every adult should have a clear understanding of where to draw the line and be prepared to ask for help. It is suggested that this should be when the result of intervening outweighs the result of not intervening.

La Vigna model

Another method that might be adopted is the La Vigna model of which there are four components:

Environment change – focuses on introducing change in the environment which makes appropriate behaviour more likely.

Teaching new skills – focuses on identifying the intent of the behaviour and teaching alternative ways of achieving the same ends, enabling the young person to get their needs met in acceptable/appropriate ways.

Reinforcement – focuses on effective methods of increasing good behaviour and making inappropriate behaviour less likely.

Reactive strategies – strategies which are used to manage inappropriate behaviour at the time it occurs. La Vigna calls this situational management.

Environmental change

Young people's needs may be physical, emotional or social and consist of factors in the following areas:

- *physical;* premises, lighting, noise, crowding, temperature
- *use of time;* choices, predictable, relevance, involvement, difficulty of task, learning styles, transitions

- *interpersonal;* social interactions, quality and quantity of relationships, respect and dignity, grouping arrangements, peer groups, ability to express needs

- *personal state;* anxiety, low self-esteem, sadness, feelings of rejection, frustration, tiredness, physical health, confidence.

Teaching new skills

The most innovative aspect of the La Vigna model is probably the emphasis it places on the communicative function of difficult behaviour. Before responding to difficult behaviour one should stop and ask what is this behaviour all about? What does this behaviour mean from the young person's perspective? Martin Herbert argues:

> *"Young people are invariably trying to solve a problem rather than be one. Their solutions to problems are often misguided because their concept of the problem is false or because their skills leave much to be desired."*

Within the behaviour there is a message which needs identifying. The message may be about the goals the young person is trying to achieve by engaging in this (unacceptable) behaviour. The emphasis here is that problem behaviour is a function of learning. This is the coping strategy that the young person has developed over time in response to their experiences albeit that it may be ineffective in getting needs met appropriately.

As one colleague said *"I didn't realise that when a young person said that it was stupid and a waste of time what they really meant was that they couldn't do it or hadn't understood. Once I realised that, I was better able to cope with and/or avoid these difficult situations."* The basic hypothesis then is that the behaviour represents a communication, the young person is demonstrating a need.

Functionally equivalent skills which would be acceptable or appropriate behaviour to enable the young person to achieve the same goal are necessary. In this case knowing that to ask if not sure is a strength not a weakness. Functionally related skills are those skills that the young person may need to be taught in order to use the alternative behaviour, for example tips on how to go about communicating.

Reinforcement

For some young people (and adults!) any attention is better than none. Sometimes adults unwittingly reward bad behaviour and fail to give reward or recognition to the appropriate behaviour. This may be felt as punishment. Unacceptable behaviour receives a great deal of attention and can then be perceived as having positive consequences.

Reactive strategies

The previous areas have focused on bringing about positive behaviour changes for the young person. Such a process will not, of course, work overnight. It will take time for the young person to learn new skills and new behaviour patterns. In the interim it will be necessary to have planned strategies for responding to unacceptable behaviour.

Reactive strategies are not about improvements in behaviour but managing immediate situations in a way which seeks to avoid escalation into more difficult situations. Any reactive strategy used should not be more intrusive than necessary to prevent escalation and avoid potentially difficult or dangerous behaviour occurring. In other words go for the lowest level of intervention necessary to bring the behaviour under control. This may be constantly scanning the group or observing the young person individually, picking up early signs of difficulty and reacting to the emerging difficult behaviour with first level responses such as:

non-verbal signal	eye contact, frown, glare
close proximity	simply moving closer to the young person
redirection/reward/praise	that looks interesting, well done, shall we try …
active listening	not assuming you always know what the difficulties are but genuinely listening to the young person's views and reflecting their feelings back to them
humour	NOT sarcasm
relocating	suggest he or she moves to another seat/area
ignoring	sometimes ignoring the situation is the best strategy but being aware of early signs of escalation is vital.

What is important is that a plan is in place for responding to unwanted/ undesirable behaviour. All members of any team must be aware and in agreement with this plan which will give consistency of approach and the young people will then know where they stand. The key objective of a reactive strategy is to provide quick and easy control. Reactive strategy is only successful if the proactive strategies are in place with the aim of teaching the young person new patterns of behaviour that will ultimately replace the inappropriate behaviour.

Recap

It is possible to reduce inappropriate behaviour by:

- preventing the behaviour in the first place by arranging the environment so that opportunities for misbehaviour are minimised
- seeing what the aim of the problem behaviour is and replacing it by alternative methods of achieving this that are easier for the young person and socially acceptable.

The ABCDE analysis

Planning an intervention

The ABC analysis is widely used as a coping strategy. David Leadbetter and Robin Trewartha in *Handling Aggression and Violence at Work*, Russell House Publishing, have extended this further as ABCDE. This strategy can be developed and used in behaviour management:

A: **Antecedents** – looking at what caused or causes the difficult behaviour and also looking at when the young person is well behaved

B: **Behaviour** – what exactly was the behaviour?

C: **Consequences** – how did the behaviour affect the young person and how did it affect others around them?

D: **Design** – help the young person to design a plan to avoid the behaviour in the future. The action plan sheet used on p.105 could also be used here

E: **Enter** – enter into positive ongoing dialogue with the young person.

Research

John Triseliotis says that success is more likely when professionals are:

- working in partnership with agencies such as education, housing, police, health, social services to develop joint strategies
- providing planned and consistent individual and family work based on a shared definition of problems and expectations.
- paying attention to practical, behavioural and personal needs
- prepared to challenge young people to own their behaviour provided a positive relationship exists
- giving regular feedback and reviews, including the re-examination and resetting of goals
- linking the young person, where needed, to groups or other activities
- accessing specialist and other flexible facilities

(*Teenagers and the Social Work Services*, John Triseliotis, Mooria Borland, Malcolm Hill and Lydia Lambert, HMSO 1995.)

Ruth Sinclair from her research entitled *Social Work Assessment with Adolescents* for the National Children's Bureau felt that certain factors influenced positive outcomes. These and the author's observations (in italics) are shown below:

- **Continuity** of input from social worker – *however, this is true of any of the professions. A young person who has a variety of teachers or schools, always sees a different doctor or who has many and varied fathers in the house will not have stability in their life.*
- **Persistence** by the social worker in pursuing objectives and advocating on behalf of the young person – *all young people need someone to speak up on their behalf; to challenge; to persevere and ensure the young person's rights are met.*
- **In-depth involvement** with the young person and their family – *all work with young people should consider both the views and feelings of the young person but also the views and feelings of the parent(s). It is vitally important that this work is not tokenistic and is carried out in a spirit of partnership.*

→

> - **A lack of dependence** on contributions from professionals from other agencies – *many people working with adolescents do not have the confidence to try to resolve a situation themselves and take recourse to others for advice/assistance. Young people may choose to confide in a particular person or may feel comfortable with that person and will prefer that individual to handle the situation themselves.*

Behaviour management

If the young person's behaviour is not acceptable, how should it be handled? Shouting or reprimanding will not change anything, especially if the behaviour is in the company of peers.

Ask to see the young person at a convenient time. Practising teachers may say that this is unrealistic but if a positive outcome is the aim then the young person must be with you rather than against you. If the meeting is called when a football or singing practice is on or their favourite TV programme is showing, then they will feel resentment before they start. The immediate end of the school/college/work day is not a good time for a meeting. Try to give the young person several alternatives from which to choose. Without proper planning, a meeting can easily get out of control. The following charts and notes may help prioritise thoughts before the meeting. They could also be used as a basis for the meeting itself.

How often does it happen that the influence of others affects our own views of what is and is not acceptable? It might be politicians, the media, our next door neighbour or, of course, our partner. It is therefore important to think about exactly **what** is unacceptable behaviour and how that differs from what you are in fact getting. If the difference is negligible it will often be better to take no action, merely making a note of the occasion in case something similar occurs in the future.

We all have different values, different prejudices, different standards. Before confronting a young person's unacceptable behaviour it is necessary to think about why the young person has behaved in a particular way. For example, a young person may eat with their mouth open, chomping their food and talking at the same time – perfectly acceptable behaviour in their own home but not necessarily so in the dining area. Should the young person be told?

Encouraging Positive Behaviour

Clarify your concern
Define what you are getting
Specify what you want

Is the difference important?

Yes   Not very different   No ——— No action

What are the obstacles to improved behaviour?
 	
Is the young person's positive behaviour praised?
 	
Is the young person's behaviour causing problems to others?
 	
Does the young person gain from unacceptable behaviour i.e. your attention, the attention of others?
	Does it matter to the young person?
	
	Does the young person know why better behaviour is important?
	
	Has the young person done it before?
	
	Has the behaviour recently/ suddenly changed?
	
	Does the young person appreciate the problems it may be causing others?
	
	Does the young person have the potential for improvement?
		Why different?
		
		Only different to you?
		
		Only different to others?
		
		Different backgrounds
		  – expectations
		  – assumptions
		  – principles
		  – prejudices

If yes, then when? Certainly not at the meal table in front of others. Some would say we should not impose our own class values on the young people. Young people themselves will tell you they want to know how to behave to help them in the future. Another young person may say that this is …!!! when what they really mean is *'I can't do it'*, *'I need help'*. They lack confidence.

The following word chart shows how difficult it is to understand young people:

Words – any of the set of words from the left hand column will go with any set of words from the right hand column e.g. a young person who rants and raves may be unsure, worried or just doesn't understand.

refuses to do something	can't do something
says it's stupid	doesn't understand
won't speak	doesn't know what/how to say
rants and raves	is embarrassed
acts the fool	is unsure
gets angry	needs attention
shows off	is worried

At a local college it was discovered that many students had never used a cup with a saucer. The student council decided that at some point in their college career every young person should be given an opportunity to drink from a cup which had its own saucer and also to eat from a set table with food displayed well. The young people would then have had the experience which, if needed, would hold them in good stead in the future.

The following are other examples where behaviour may differ but the young person may be unaware that their behaviour or action is unacceptable. Explanations and reasons may be all that is required:

- swearing
- drinking from a bottle
- keeping boots/shoes on in the house
- putting feet up on chairs
- washing hands before/after using the toilet
- rushing to go through the door in front of others or letting the door slam
- respecting a person for what they are regardless of their sex, sexual orientation, religion, race, culture, disability or ability

Young people will also have varying morals about the same subject in differing circumstances. For example they may see nothing wrong in stealing from shops or other people, yet if their granny was robbed the young person might well beat-up the thief and quite soon after decry violent behaviour at football matches.

So what can be done? It is essential young people have opportunities to experience new situations, understand and be tolerant of other people's cultures and way of life; visit new places, have new challenges; take part in discussions. In this way they will learn from these experiences and develop their own principles and beliefs and at the same time learn to respect those of others.

Until it is discovered why a young person behaves in a particular way, all the control in the world will have little effect if it is aimed in the wrong direction. A note should be made of when difficulties have occurred before to see if there is a pattern. For example, a young person may be agitated say every Tuesday after school (she hates maths!) or on say a Thursday (his mother's boyfriend stays the night). It is also important to make a note of when a young person is not being difficult. You can then speak to them positively and look for ways of lessening the difficult behaviour.

Young people should be encouraged to discuss:

- their behaviour and others behaviour
- right and wrong
- what is acceptable and what is not
- what control they think is needed and why
- what sanctions should be imposed, how and by whom
- relationships with others such as parents, carers, teachers, friends and why they might feel aggressive towards them; frightened of them; imposed on/by them

It is important for young people to learn to be responsible for their own behaviour.

During a research project undertaken for the University of Oxford (*How to Stay out of Trouble*, A Buchanan et al), persistent young offenders were interviewed. When posed with the question of what might make them re-offend, over 90% ticked either or both boxes highlighting **boredom** or **nothing to do in the day**.

If this small sample is typical, then there is a need to start helping young people to:

- find out what interests them
- what facilities/resources are available
- what they can do on their own, with others, with adults
- what the initial outlay/ongoing outlay is likely to be and if there are any funds available.

Young people may need help to get started and many will need help to continue. They will need praise; opportunities to succeed (and fail, providing they can be helped to see the positives from the failure); encouragement and someone to show an interest. They need to learn to be creative, resourceful, to use their own initiative and to take responsibility for their own lives.

One thing that is important is that whilst it is fine introducing young people to activities such as 10-pin bowling or skating so they know what is possible, the cost is often prohibitive. They should also be introduced, therefore, to other activities which do not incur expenditure and with which they will be able to continue later in life such as walking and cycling.

Many young people will say they do not like doing particular things. This may be because they have failed in the past, they think others will laugh at them, they have been put down or bullied, or they think they are not good enough or clever enough. Aggressive behaviour or refusal to participate may also be a cover for lack of confidence. They will need support, encouragement, time and effort but it will be worth it when they gain a sense of achievement from participation.

If a young person has broken the law then it is obvious to them that their behaviour causes problems to others. However, the vast majority will either never offend or will only offend once in their life. Many of these young people will behave at times in a manner which others find unacceptable or causes problems to others. A young person may be totally unaware of this and someone taking the time and trouble to explain things to them will be all that is required. On the other hand the behaviour may be a deliberate or sometimes subconscious, way of gaining attention. The underlying reasons for this then need to be investigated.

Telling young people what they have done and what they should do instead is not enough. Young people need to know why certain behaviour is unacceptable and why better behaviour is important. It is no good saying *"If you work hard at school you'll get a good job when you leave"* when the reality is that in your particular location the chance of a 16 year old getting any sort of job is almost nil and the young person knows it. The explanation must be realistic and true.

Strategies for promoting good behaviour

All-the-time strategies

When dealing with issues concerning adolescent behaviour the following principles may help:

Be supportive

Avoid making the adolescent feel inadequate – but set clear standards of performance. High performance standards are a positive motivator.

Keep it impersonal

The easiest thing in the world is to attack the person when confronting an issue. Avoid this by focussing on the problem – even if the person *is* the problem. *"I don't have a problem with you – but I do have a problem with what you are doing."*

Be specific about the problem

Defining the right problem may be hard work, and a discussion may cover several problems, but if the wrong problem is defined the wrong solution follows.

Handle problems one at a time

If you think the adolescent is the problem, focus on the results of their behaviour.

Keep an open mind

Don't assume the **cause** of a problem until you have all the **facts**. Some of the facts will only come to light if you **listen** to the young person. We all make genuine mistakes, but if you assume the young person has deliberately done wrong you are likely to act accordingly – with a **closed** mind.

Making assumptions can damage your relationships. It is reasonable and sensible to have suspicions. **Suspect** what you like, that is fair enough – but avoid pursuing suspicions too hard. As you look for a solution you will discover whether or not your suspicions are well founded.

Specify the requirements

Encourage the young person to comment and to make suggestions. Ask, *"What do you think?"* **Listening** encourages people to express their opinions and make suggestions – but it can be hard work. **Not listening** shuts them up.

When encouraging suggestions, be ready to build on part-ideas. Accept that you can't have all the answers. If you do all the thinking you are doing the young person's work for them – it is much better if they work things out for themselves – with your help! Watch out for clues to potential problems – opinions expressed obliquely may be a sign. If probed or questioned they may then reveal ideas for solutions. Opinions about **your** suggestions may reveal objections or possible snags.

Don't rush for a solution

Allow the young person adequate time to think things through. Lasting solutions take time and this is important with something new. By planning ahead, you can allow time for the young person to seek information, work on alternatives – or just **think**. The time allowed should suit the circumstances; it might be five minutes or five weeks – or it might be five seconds. Not allowing time will be counter-productive. Also **you** will need time to think through the problem, so if a discussion is going nowhere you should be prepared to adjourn it.

Agree actions and dates

Here the emphasis is on **action** and **completion targets**. The **adult** must ensure the action programme is **appropriate** for the young person in the circumstances at that time. It **may** be appropriate for the young person to do nothing – but this must be by arrangement not by default.

When there is no action programme for the young person – check to see if **they** should be doing some of the things **you** have promised to do. If you miss this step, you could each finish up thinking the other will take action – and nothing gets done.

Always set a review date
This gives a deadline – without which the task may be deferred or forgotten. The date may be specific, i.e. a diary date or it may be based around an event – *"let me know after you've seen the doctor"*. The second alternative shifts responsibility **to the young person** (but doesn't stop you checking if you want to) and it gives discretion. Switching from a diary date to an event date indicates a more mature working relationship.

Praising good behaviour

Most adolescents behave in an acceptable way most of the time but often it is only the perceived bad behaviour that is commented upon or is considered to require some attention. Often a young person will say of their mentor, *"he is quick enough to jump on you when you do something wrong, but never says anything all the time things are OK"*. Yet, given that adolescents behave well a lot of the time it should be easy to praise a piece of good behaviour (positive stroking). So, good motivators make time to catch people doing something right – then praise them for it (*The One Minute Manager*, Kenneth Blanchard and Spencer Johnson, Fontana Books).

Commenting favourably on good behaviour helps to keep the occasional problem in perspective. And when you praise a young person about the benefits of behaving in a specific way you are, at the same time, reinforcing the standards you require. That reinforcement should be a constant process which also reminds young people **why** they are doing what they are doing. Most people shy away from giving praise because they feel that it should not be necessary (not true) or because they feel uncomfortable about doing it in case they embarrass themselves or the young person. The suggested way of going about praising is as follows.

Tell the young person specifically what he or she has done which deserves praise, and **why**. Make it clear to the young person that you genuinely appreciate what they have done. Watch their response carefully as this may give a clue to other issues that need addressing – you may hear about an idea that the young person has been mulling over; or of concerns he or she may not have had the courage to voice; perhaps an opinion about your behaviour. You may at this point be confronted by an adverse reaction or outright complaint. So long as you are prepared for this reaction and have a method for dealing with it, this is a positive sign. You are actually communicating and have a chance of resolving an issue.

Handling a complaint

Handling a complaint from a young person is not the same as 'giving in' to it – that may not be appropriate. A complaint or problem which appears quite small to an adult may be very serious to an adolescent. In such cases it might not be the problem itself which is important but the way in which it is handled. Insensitive handling can lead to problems growing out of all proportion – or to the adult missing important feedback or information. A loudly made complaint may be intended to intimidate the adult or to cover up the young person's own nervousness – or fear of rejection. However a gentle complaint may still be a determined one – also needing good handling.

To manage successfully the problem or complaint make sure you follow these steps:

Resolving problems

Give the young person your full attention – use your interviewing/questioning skills to prompt the young person to keep talking. Listen for possible clues then check them out using probe questions. Make notes – it shows that you are serious about understanding the problem – key words will do – and summarise in your own words. In this way you encourage the young person to put you right if there is any misunderstanding. It is important at this stage to establish how the young person feels about the problem – don't just concentrate on what is said.

Reassure the young person that he or she was right to raise the issue and show that you understand their feelings – be aware that feelings may be more important than facts and together they indicate the total problem to be handled. Note though that understanding feelings is **not** agreeing with or condoning them. The young person may be reluctant to reveal their feelings directly; or may be unsure about what they want from you. Putting yourself in their shoes and **showing** you know what it feels like – is vital for full understanding. Remember – feelings may be half the problem. Reassuring, however low key, will calm a situation.

State your own position undefensively and without hostility (do not accrue black stamps). You may not know your position – you may need time to think things through. Your position might be simple or quite complex. Do not react badly, and do not try to justify the unjustifiable. Going on the defensive leads to counter-attack and to a problem of credibility (black stamps).

There is no harm in an apology if appropriate, nor an expression of regret. You both need to know where you stand as in this way you have a joint platform for moving forward.

Get ideas and suggestions from the young person – sometimes the young person may be just waiting to be asked (complaining about the present situation may be seen as the only way to make a suggestion). At other times they may need to be encouraged, through careful exploration, to think through the problem and suggest a solution. The suggestions could be for **you** to take some action – using resources which only you control. If the young person insists, and then objects to your proposed solution, state that it is **your** problem and you can simply ask for suggestions. Any outrageous ideas can easily be related back to your stated position.

Agree what will happen next – this may be independent of the young person's suggestions. It may be a little or a lot but – **only** if it is applicable. Usually, the more that people can do to solve their own problems the better – for their own self-esteem and development, and for your workload. Even if the adult can only promise to 'look into' something the setting of a follow-up date for reporting back will ensure that nothing is left to fester. Conversely, no follow-up date speaks for itself.

Managing change

This is about getting the young person to accept a new idea or to change current behaviour. Adolescence is a continuous change process. Every change presents an opportunity for communication and co-operation – or conflict. Some young people will be keen to develop new skills and knowledge –

others will react differently depending upon their background, experience, peer group attitudes, ability to learn or perceived risks. It is essential to prepare for this natural and perfectly normal resistance and to act accordingly. By following these steps you can ensure genuine consultation and participation:

Be clear about your objectives – specifically what are you aiming to achieve with the change, and why? Is it a firm idea, or a vague idea? Do you want the young person to think about it or to give it a go? Also do you want full agreement or only an initial reaction? Do you need a detailed action plan?

Also consider how your proposal will affect the young person in terms of freedom, choice, money, personal interests, budgets, and so on? Are there alternatives? If an alternative is offered will you consider it and what discretion do you have to change the proposal?

Explain in detail why the change is necessary – with information young people can contribute to the change, even persuade others that the change is a good idea. Without information there can be no real understanding or commitment to the idea. This action involves the young person and gives you the chance to show them where you stand in terms of enthusiasm, commitment, firmness and/or willingness to be flexible.

Explain the proposal in detail and the implications for the young person – to do this successfully you will have had to think the idea through from the young person's point of view – not just your own. You will be aware of the plus points and the minus points and all should be mentioned. For the minuses there should be some balancing pluses to which you can refer – if not is it such a good idea in the first place?

In some cases a practical demonstration will be appropriate where you teach the young person the new method or procedure. At this stage consider the whole range of communication tools to get your point across, e.g. drawings, plans, a check-list, figures, a visit – or a separate learning activity. Give the young person time to absorb the new method or procedure. Make sure you test understanding by seeing the young person actually **do** things correctly using the new method or procedure. Now identify and recognise any new problems. Ask the young person how they feel about the new way. Listen to their comments.

This step is the difficult one where you will need to manage the objections – some emotional and some perhaps irrational. Remember – resistance to change is legitimate, so you must listen well and empathise. The young person must be able to raise anything he or she wants – progress comes later. Make sure you fully understand any objection and, more importantly, the feelings behind it. Make a note so that it can then be handled as a problem in the next step. Recognising new problems connected with the change means acknowledging their validity.

Together work out ways around the difficulties – ask for ideas for overcoming any problems and implementing the change. At this step the adult, with a better picture of likely problems, may decide to adjourn to give the young person time to reflect on benefits and to see problems in perspective – before trying to get an action plan. Also at this point it might be appropriate to modify the proposal as a result of what arose earlier.

Note that there is no mention of gaining agreement. The method seeks agreement but sometimes you may have to push ahead without it.

Action plan

A way to help young people become responsible for their own actions is to jointly produce an action plan.

What can be done?

What can he or she do?

Agreed action plan

Their suggestions   Your suggestions

Timescale   Feedback   Discussion   Monitor

What can a young person do to improve their behaviour – their suggestions/ your suggestions? If the plan has the young person's commitment then it is much more likely to succeed. It is also important to set realistic targets.

A young lad was misbehaving at school in all sorts of ways. Various solutions were tried without success. Then he was set just two small targets to achieve for the first week – to wear his school tie and bring a pen every day. He had to report to his tutor before school and after school to check that his targets had been met, thus ensuring he also attended school and was learning to be responsible by remembering to report back to the tutor after school. The following week he also brought something to write on and his lesson timetable, then his P.E. kit and so on.

This very simple scheme was successful because it had the commitment of the boy, his parents, the teacher and the head. A record was kept of his progress which was praised and the lad could see what he was capable of achieving without losing face with anyone. Regular discussion took place without hostilities and the lad went on to achieve his potential at GCSE level in the school.

An action plan (sample on following page) should show:
- what has been agreed
- timescale
- who is to do what
- agreement to meet regularly and set first date
- how progress is to be monitored
- future plans.

Together the chapters on Successful communication and Care and control provide a wide variety of approaches for working with young people. These will not automatically work immediately or all the time. What is needed is to practise getting the communication right and then learning the theories and developing them to suit your own personality. The confidence of having strategies available for a wide variety of situations will improve your chances of success.

Individual action plan

Name: Date commenced:

                                         Date completed:

Those involved in constructing this plan:

Current behaviour causing concern:

Target(s) for change: Success criteria:

Environmental changes to be made:

Preventative measures to be taken:

Strategies to reinforce the targets:

Agreed strategies for responding to unacceptable behaviour in the interim:

Date to meet to look at success of plan and those to be invited to meeting:

Agreed action following meeting:

Any other comments:

Young person's comments:

Chapter 8

Education

Young people who experience problems within the education system may be going through a 'normal' adolescent phase or may be experiencing a specific difficulty. As young people are meant to be in school for something like 30 hours per week carrying out activities they may neither enjoy nor see the relevance of, it is not surprising that from time to time they cause problems. Other young people who may be described as 'in need' will either be 'in care'; disturbed; have difficult home lives; live in poverty, lack parental support or control or may just have particularly difficult problems coping with school.

The first part of this chapter is in the form of a brief paper outlining some strategies. Any one working with young people should advocate for them, agitate for change and ensure that these strategies are implemented.

The second part of the chapter looks at some ideas that have been developed recently to help others through their school careers and to help them achieve their educational potential. These are:

- the Schools Council work on developing pupil potential
- peer mediation in bullying
- school counselling
- mentoring schemes
- educational therapy
- early intervention
- developing a positive work culture
- developing portage and highscope schemes for use with older young people;
- positive parting action group.

Many of these can easily be adapted for use in schools and in other establishments such as children's homes, youth clubs and drop-in centres. There may also be funding available from a variety of sources to assist with the implementation of some of these schemes.

This chapter should not in any way be seen to criticise the excellent work that is already taking place. It should be seen as a positive way of extending the debate and hopefully improving the education of young people by developing a unified approach to their education. The following are some comments from the young people about school and teachers, in no particular order:

- Don't listen.
- Too many supply teachers.
- To suspend you is a holiday.
- To suspend you is the easy option.
- Teachers won't stick up for you.
- I hate being in a room on my own.
- I don't like being in large groups.
- I can't handle hassle and stress because of my family.
- We're second class citizens.
- Home tutor – not enough lessons.
- No discipline.
- Won't take you for what you are.

Education paper

Education provision for young people, just like health provision, varies dramatically from area to area. In a secure unit when the young offenders are asked what they like about the place invariably the reply is education. Most of these young people had been excluded from school long before they had offended.

Many local authorities and other voluntary organisations are involved in schemes to attempt to improve the education of young people. However, figures are still being published showing the lack of educational achievement. In some local authority areas many of the points mentioned in the following pages are in operation. What is needed is a national strategic plan for all, which is monitored regularly and the person responsible being given authority to ensure full implementation.

Education should mean education in the widest sense. This should not only be educational and life skills but making and keeping friends, education for free time, coping alone and parenting, housekeeping and budgeting skills. It should also cover learning about morals, ethics and acceptable standards of behaviour. Twenty years ago most of these were taught as an integral part of the teaching day.

The academic syllabus with its prescriptive requirements means that in most schools every effort is made to ensure young people achieve their appropriate academic levels regardless of circumstance. It is great that every young person should learn a foreign language but not if their reading and first language skills are so poor that there is no opportunity for them to catch up.

In America there are many compensatory education schemes being advocated. In this country too ad hoc schemes are being developed to improve the education of young people. These include Saturday morning clubs, work on reducing truancy, the use of education social workers as well as/instead of education welfare officers, interactive videos, open learning and computers both in and out of school.

Many schools already use IT (information technology) to lesser and greater degrees but many resources are sadly under-utilised in school. This equipment should be available for young people to use for educational purposes both before and after school and during breaks and lunchtimes. Young people whose numeracy and literacy skills need improving should be given priority of use. Many further education colleges report the success of using such alternatives. Young people can experience achieving their goals or repeating something they do not understand at their own pace without ridicule from the rest of the group and moving on at a pace appropriate to each individual.

European Union funding for 'Second Chance Schools' has been accepted. These will be for young unemployed 16 to 24 year-olds without qualifications to learn the basics such as core literacy, numeracy and workplace skills using methods different from those that failed them the first time around.

All these schemes have much to commend them and are an important step in the right direction. However, certain barriers also need to be broken down before young people can achieve their educational potential:

Emotional barriers – research shows that 20 per cent of all young people experience special educational needs at some point in their school life. It is in the definition of special education needs that the difficulty arises. A special educational needs (SEN) teacher said recently that she had a young person in her group who appeared to exhibit learning difficulties, similar to the young person's two older brothers. When the teacher tested the young person, her educational ability came out as 'normal'. However, because of the emotional trauma she had experienced she had never indicated such ability.

The first point then is that young people may have special educational needs solely for **emotional reasons**. This may be manifested as problem behaviour, poor concentration or apparent low ability.

Priority barriers – the second point concerns **priorities**. Different people have different priorities.

Social Services priorities

Answering Back (Buchanan et al.) recommends that a young person should not, other than in exceptional circumstances or if sick, be out of school for more than three days. A very experienced social care manager stated quite plainly that this recommendation was wrong – *"You've got to remember that many of the young people I deal with will have been abused and would not be able to cope with school."* If a young person has been abused and taken away from home, school may be the one place where that young person can normalise his or her life. It may be the place where their friends are, where adults they know and trust are and where they can carry out tasks which may help them to forget albeit briefly their experiences.

Schools' priorities:

Schools often think certain young people may damage the reputation of the school. This is particularly true if the young person has been in trouble with the law. With the publication of statistics, schools may no longer wish to accept trouble makers. Many young people will have had a disturbed educational background so may well be underachieving having changed schools many times. Again their lack of educational attainment will lower the school's overall statistics. To avoid poor attendance and high truancy rates some schools are excluding more and more young people.

Expectation barriers – whose expectations?

1. **Social workers** – social workers are very busy people and placing a young person in a suitable home is often their main priority. A foster carer told of a recent experience where she was asked to take a problem teenager who had a history of stealing and violence. This carer asked for the young person's education plan. There was not one: the carer said she felt she could cope with the lad providing he was being educated as he would then have something to work for and work towards. Sadly there was no education provision for this boy and he did not go to this excellent foster home.

2. **Residential workers** – very often these workers are so concerned with maintaining discipline and standards of behaviour that they do not expect sufficiently high standards of educational achievement or attendance at school from their clients.

3. **Foster carers** – by their nature are caring people but sometimes they are so concerned about the physical and emotional well-being of the young person that education is low down the list of priorities provided there is not a problem at school.

4. **Parents** – some parents of young people may well have low educational expectations of their children having failed the education system themselves. Conversely some parents have far too high expectations and are often unwittingly setting their children up to fail.

5. **Young people** – many young people often have low self-esteem and lack confidence.

6. **Teachers** – teachers should have the highest possible realistic expectations for their students.

From negative to positive

Everyone must have high expectations of young people. By changing attitudes, enhancing awareness, effectively using existing facilities and gaining the commitment of everyone involved with the young person success can be achieved.

Schools should:

- provide lively interesting and relevant lessons for everyone in stimulating environments
- should evolve new courses and work programmes specially designed/adapted for particular young people
- look at ways to make lessons hidden and change methods of assessment as at present most of these require age related reading
- make greater use of different teaching methods including information technology
- ensure what is taught is relevant.

Schools should also:

- give extra help to enable young people to catch up
- provide a structured learning environment. This is particularly important for young people whose lives have been disordered
- explain to young people why education is important and not assume they know
- praise progress, no matter how slow or small
- reward success, once out of fashion, but now gaining in popularity as many people realise that young people, just like adults, like to feel they have earned something for their effort
- ensure the young person is not bullied or treated differently because of their circumstances, colour, race, religion or disability
- ensure the young person is not underachieving
- ensure homework is set, corrected and returned regularly
- have positive attitudes for all young people. A conversation was overheard on a train recently where the teacher said *"sit down, shut up and listen"*. Young people confirm that sadly all too often this attitude prevails
- advise young people of what is possible. This advice must be realistic but the expectation must be high. They should also be advised of what is needed to achieve their potential which may also mean explaining what the different qualifications and levels mean and what the different courses entail.

In procedures schools should:

- provide a stable environment – unfortunately schools are often having to resort to the use of a large number of supply teachers. Job-share is another example which in theory works very well but in practice means the young person has many different teachers. When an 11 year old goes to secondary school they may well have 15 different teachers and 10 different rooms in one week. This will be stressful for any young person but particularly for a young person whose life has been disordered and who especially needs stability
- welcome the parent/carer/social worker into the school and work closely with everyone involved with the young person ensuring they realise that their contribution is necessary
- let someone know immediately something does not seem quite right.

No one should be excluded from school unless alternative educational arrangements have been made.

Schools should also:

- nominate one teacher, with special responsibility for young people who may be exhibiting difficult behaviour or appear to be having problems
- provide an advocate or mentor for the young person in whom they can confide. This person may be a paid classroom assistant or a volunteer who comes into the school
- for older young people schools should work closely with careers and further education people to ensure the young person is well advised on possible careers and on the appropriateness of chosen college courses
- schools should use existing resources to the full, e.g. units.

Being on report – many schools run a scheme of putting young people on report if they have misbehaved. This means at the beginning of each day the young person must get their form teacher/tutor to sign their form. Everyone who teaches them throughout the day must sign to say they have behaved well and then the tutor signs the form at the end of the day. The parent/carer signs the form in the evening. This is not just a way to discipline young people, it is also a way of giving them attention which after all may be what they are seeking. A similar scheme can operate in a children's home. For example a young person who has misbehaved is set achievable goals for say a week, thus rewarding success rather than giving sanctions.

Use of facilities – maximum use should be made of school buildings at weekends, after school and during the holidays. After school clubs and activities should be an essential part of **every** school. Everyone should have quiet places to do homework, to be warm and to have interested adults around. This will help develop a positive attitude to school.

The use of units

These may be known by other names in different regions and are places for young people who have been excluded from mainstream school – 'snooker and drugs' is how one carer described the unit many of the young people she looks after attend. Poor units as with poor schools should have no place in the education of young people. As in all walks of life these units do vary from place to place. Two visited recently both had much to commend them but each was remarkably different in its approach.

The first unit had a very relaxed atmosphere. The young people were involved in all areas of decision making. When they arrived they could make coffee and toast, they were asked what they wanted for lunch – within a very limited budget of course. They learn practical skills like mending the radio in the minibus or house decorating as well as having basic education lessons.

The second unit was highly structured. When they join the unit the young people are given a contract to sign covering such things as regular attendance and punctuality, treating each other with courtesy and respect, being clean and tidy, remaining on-site for the whole school day, as well as working to the best of their ability, especially when faced with a challenging situation. The young people have a timetable which includes normal lessons, visiting speakers, work experience, educational visits, individual and group counselling.

One problem which does occur is that units are often for all young people. This means that a quite innocent 11 year old may be influenced by older more street wise young people. Specialist teachers are obviously necessary.

Units should not be seen as the last resort but should be utilised more. Staff at both the units said that **early referral** gives the best chance of success. The dilemma then is should other young people be put in a unit with small groups and very personal attention but separated from the majority of young people of their own age? Alternatively should every effort be made to normalise them as far as possible? The answer is that young people may need a combination of both a unit and mainstream schooling for some period in their school life, similar to the nurture schemes for younger children already in operation in some areas. Planned programmes should be set up in joint consultation with schools and units.

The suggestion is an adaptation of this. When a young person first joins the school an educational assessment should be made if no educational records are immediately available. An IEP (individual education plan) should be drawn up – similar to that produced for SEN young people.

- If the young person is behind in any area of work then they could go to the unit for part of the day where personalised tuition would help them catch up.
- If they have difficulty concentrating they can receive help for this.
- Behavioural and emotional problems can be dealt with at the unit.
- If the young person has not been in school for some time then a planned programme can be made to help them back into school with the smaller groups in the unit making this easier.
- If during the young person's time back in the normal classroom the young person feels totally unable to cope, then provision should be made for the young person to go back to the unit for a short time. The young person should, of course, tell the teacher and also sign a form giving time, date and reason for leaving the classroom. This form can then be monitored closely. It may well be that a pattern builds up and the young person can be further helped.
- Weekly progress meetings should take place with the young person and whoever is designated to be responsible for the young person. The meetings should gradually be reduced in frequency until the young person is back in full-time mainstream education.

The use of these units should be seen as a positive step in the emotional and educational development of the young person and the notion of 'sin bin' should have no place in any school.

Working with excluded young people

In *Experiences of Youth* the following suggestions have been made for those working with excluded young people. However, much of this is essential for all work with adolescents:

- young people need to be cared for and respected as individuals
- young people need to see some real value in attending school.

Adults should realise:

- that undisciplined pupils are not missed from school
- their absence may be welcomed by hard-pressed teachers
- you have to want them to succeed if you are going to work with them effectively
- together you must create meaningful personal objectives
- the need to develop clear ideas about sanctions, incentives and working boundaries
- most young people will need help to improve their self-identity and sense of self-worth in addition to improving their basic skills in literacy and numeracy
- most young people will need plenty of opportunities for achievement and help with improving their confidence, communication skills and general strengths and weaknesses.

Local authorities should in all cases:

- ensure that education and social services departments work closely together
- heighten the awareness of all those working with young people of the importance of a young person's education
- make financial provision for extra tuition to ensure each young person has the opportunity to catch up and achieve their true potential
- run all meetings, to which young people are invited, out of school hours
- ensure that anyone taking a young person out of school should have a very good reason for so doing

- speed up educational decisions. A guardian ad litem panel manager said recently that a very good foster home had been found for a young person but they was unable to be so placed, because of the delay in obtaining an educational decision

- ensure schools are given a certain amount of freedom and flexibility, including providing support staff, both qualified and unqualified, to develop educational programmes including vocational courses which may be more appropriate for some young people.

If a young person is in 'care', local authorities responsible for the children's home should:

- Nominate and **train** at least one person in every children's home to be responsible for the education of all those in the home. This person should not be the field social worker. They should help with homework as necessary or find someone else who can help. The young person will then know that there is someone who is interested and who will listen if they wish to talk about their educational achievements or just about their day at school.

- Employ one person in children's homes who should be responsible for overseeing an education programme for the residents in the home. This person could also be the one foster carers or fostered young people can contact if they need advice, help or information on education in the area.

- Ensure that an up-to-date computer, compatible with local schools, is available in every children's home and that a member of staff is qualified to assist young people with computer related problems. This could also be used to improve numeracy, literacy and IT skills.

- Provide access to a computer for all young people in foster homes.

- Ensure that books and magazines are readily available at all times.

- Provide individual learning programmes using open learning, videos, members of the local community, older young people in the home, in fact any avenue of learning – let the young person help develop and thus have ownership for their own learning programme.

- Ensure that if a young person is out of school no more than 3 days should elapse before educational provision is made.

- Provide suitable places for all young people 'in care' to work quietly on their school subjects.

- Should advise of any financial assistance for education to which young people are entitled when they leave care. Someone should be appointed whom the young person can contact at any reasonable time for advice on education.

In schools generally:

- If any young person is out of school for any time for any reason work should be provided and whoever is responsible for the young person should ensure the work is done. Being out of school should not be seen as a holiday.
- Home tuition should be considered **as a short-term last resort only and should be time limited**. Home tutors should work closely with schools, both at the early sign of trouble and also in helping young people get back into school.
- Incentives should be provided for schools to avoid suspending young people.
- Additional incentives should be provided for a school to take a difficult young person where he or she has been suspended from a previous school.
- No young person should be suspended until alternative educational arrangements have been made.
- Standards should be monitored, records brought forward and acted upon. Decisions should be time-limited.

The courts should:

- ensure that a young person's educational plan is an integral part of any provision the court makes
- reduce the long waiting time and postponements of a court hearing to a minimum. It is very unsettling for a young person to be aware of a pending court hearing. This may affect concentration by not knowing when a case is going to be heard.

The parents should:

- work with all concerned in ensuring the young person achieves their potential
- attend parents evenings, visit the school when asked. Parents should feel necessary not just welcome in schools

- praise; have high expectations of the young person; show an interest
- if the parent(s) feel that because of circumstances their education is lacking they should be informed about what help is available to parents to improve their reading or numeracy. In so doing, it will help their confidence and they will better understand the difficulties a young person may be experiencing.

Other people should:

- be involved with education. There must be many people in the community who have a skill or just the ability to listen to a young person read who would be only too willing to help if they knew how to go about offering to help. Many unemployed youngsters too would be willing to help others as would older young people in the family or community. Someone must be appointed to harness this waste of goodwill.

School leavers

Young people who have left school often realise that education is after all important but think it is too late to catch up. Some suggestions for drop-in centres and other groups involved with these young people are:

- **Use IT** – there are many programmes that a young person can work through at their own pace and at their own level in areas such as numeracy; literacy; keyboard skills.
- **Numeracy and literacy schemes** – most local authorities have such schemes but these require some commitment from the young person which they may not feel able to give. Before attending these sorts of sessions they will need help in learning to make and keep promises, attend on time, bring appropriate equipment. All of which will be helpful when they are in work or looking for work.
- **'Second Chance Schools'** – as noted on p.108 it is worth checking at the local public library to see whether this or other similar schemes are in operation including open learning schemes with the local public library being the centre.
- **Young mother's schemes** – in Wiltshire a group has been set up in a local school for mothers with literacy problems who wanted to be able to read in order to help their own children. This has been

fantastically successful and the local community centre has set up a similar scheme for numeracy. Many mothers attend both sessions and funding has been found for everything except examination fees which the mothers pay towards weekly. This type of scheme does not have to be only for mothers. Another scheme in a school in Hampshire for example has obtained funding from the European Social Fund and a local college and equipped a computer room and organised courses in IT and job search skills.

- **Involving the local community and business** – this could be in the form of mentoring, helping with literacy or numeracy or providing surplus computers and other equipment such as desks and chairs.

- **Visits and visitors** – many young people say they do not want to work in an office or a factory but do not actually know what is involved. Visits to such places and being told what qualifications are needed may be just the motivation that is required.

One young person who is now learning to read offered the following advice: *"Don't be ashamed of your 3 R's problems. 'Look at your life and say I can do it'."*

Other educational schemes

These schemes that can be used or adapted for use in other locations as well as in schools.

Schools councils

School councils promote a sense of caring. They provide a structure that encourages pupils to deal with real issues which affect the benefit and welfare of the school community. It is recommended that every class should have its own elected pupils on the School Council whose aims and objectives are:

- **Charter of behaviour** – give pupils the opportunity to participate in shaping and reviewing the school's behaviour policy. This can be assisted by a collectively agreed charter of behaviour based upon a respect for rational argument and non-violent ways of resolving conflict.

- **Mutual care** – provide pupils with the opportunity to realise that they have a positive role to play in caring for each other, assist in dealing with issues such as to protect and support victims of bullying, minimise unauthorised absences and to assist in eliminating any forms of discrimination. Pupil councillors can become part of an 'early warning' system for pupils at risk and assist by mediating in pupil conflict.

- **Involving the whole school** – encourage the involvement of the whole school in the caring process whereby pupil councillors report back to their classes following council meetings, recognising the importance of ascertaining pupils' views. This will encourage discussion and involve the pupils on issues of concern within the school.

- **The school buildings** – foster a sense of ownership and care of premises and property.

- **The school community** – assist in improving the understanding, co-operation and shared values between teachers, pupils, governors and parents.

- **Initiative** – increase the involvement in pupil initiated extra curricular activities.

- **Teachers' time** – reduce the number of time wasting problems with which teachers have to deal, including often trivial incidents such as persistent disruption affecting the whole class, by selective referral to the school council.

- **Growing up** – give pupils the opportunity to develop their self-confidence, self-esteem, mutual respect, self-discipline and social responsibility. This will assist them to face the challenges of life with an active concern for human rights.

Peer mediation

The Newham Conflict and Change Project has been set up to train young people as peer mediators, or child counsellors, so they will be able to help calm tempers and resolve disputes within schools.

Mediation is a process whereby an outsider is invited by people with a dispute to help them come to a solution on which they can agree. The mediator should not have a vested interest in the outcome of the mediation as this would compromise the impartiality of the process. The key to successful mediation is that those concerned must work together to find an answer. A solution that is acceptable to only one party will not work.

Counselling in schools

In recent times the use of experts has been widely used within schools but there is now the beginning of a trend for schools to endeavour to cope themselves rather than passing the buck to others. This has meant that many teachers are being trained in counselling skills which has proved extremely successful in helping pupils.

Mentoring

The Dalston Youth Project is one of many groups which is offering young people adult mentors. The mentors and adults in this scheme meet once a fortnight and in between keep in contact by telephone. The mentors are people from similar backgrounds to the young people; open-minded, good listeners, who can be any age or sex and are volunteers. The scheme usually lasts about a year, although quite often the individuals keep in touch afterwards.

Educational therapy

Learning failure may affect self-esteem, behaviour and functioning in school. This has made the need for educational therapy paramount. Following assessment, the therapists work with individual young people and normally a psychiatric social worker. They may also work with teachers, school counsellors and special educational needs co-ordinators.

Early intervention

This is the name given to a range of interventions intended to prevent or mitigate later adverse situations. In health it can range from dietary advice and screening programmes and in education range from measures to prevent dropout and exclusion from school, improve literacy/numeracy, teach parenting or coping skills.

Portage and Highscope schemes

Portage is partnership between parents/carers and professionals in the home. The aim is to equip parents/carers with the skills and confidence they need to help their child.

The Highscope approach is one in which both adult and child plan and initiate activities and actively work together. The consistency in the organisation of an orderly and stimulating environment, daily routine and adult-child interaction based on mutual relationships of trust and respect can help young people in developing responsibility for their own learning through the plan-do-review cycle. This produces three outcomes important in developing effective adults – expressing intentions, generating experiences and reflecting upon them.

Both of these schemes while designed for younger children, especially those with special needs could be adapted in any circumstance for use with young people.

Positive parenting action group

At the Fort Hill Community School in Basingstoke parents of pupils who are causing concern are invited into the school for informal chats over a cup of tea. Ways of helping the young person, and sometimes the parent(s), are discussed and a plan is agreed between the parent, the teacher and the young person. Sometimes the teachers visit the parent(s) in their own home.

The Time Out from Education Scheme

This has been introduced in nine schools in Leeds by the police. If pupils want to leave the school during the day they have to make sure they are issued with special passes which cannot be forged or copied. Each pass bears the school logo, date, time allowed out and the pupil's name. If a youngster is found without a pass they will be questioned by the police and returned to school. Some traders in the area have started checking on pupils when they appear in their shops during lesson time. The scheme costs about £250 per year to administer and is organised in co-operation with the education welfare service which monitors school attendance levels. It is also hoped that the scheme will reduce juvenile crime.

Many young people see education as a way out of their circumstances. They do not know:

- how to go about improving their literacy/numeracy skills
- what is available to them, or even, what is possible.

They need all the help you can give them in order to achieve success in their education.

Chapter 9

Health

The aim of this chapter is not to regurgitate the contents of a wide variety of leaflets aimed at young people. These are readily available from G.P. surgeries, clinics, schools, youth clubs, community health centres and the relevant organisations themselves. The names and addresses of some of these are listed in Appendix 1. This chapter sets out to encourage a positive attitude to health as well as examining a piece of research undertaken by De Montfort University on the health needs of young people leaving care and looking at its' implication for all young people. The final part of the chapter lists some areas of health care and concern with some positive responses.

Adolescents suffer many of the same conditions as people in other age groups plus some specific conditions such as acne; worries about puberty; eating disorders, difficulties with relationships and sexual development.

The Department of Health initiative *The Health of the Young Nation* has revealed that over three-quarters of adolescents see themselves as responsible for their own health, and three-quarters also understand that the way they choose to live will influence their own health. In other words, young people know that if they smoke they may get cancer or if they have unprotected sex they may get pregnant or get HIV or AIDS. They see health as being, to some extent, a person's own responsibility and that too much health promotion, especially of the negative kind, risks overkill:

> **'Don't smoke ... drink ... take drugs ... have sex'.**

The legal age for personal responsibility for health care is 16 though the Gillick verdict on the issue of contraception for those aged under 16 years has changed the climate for this age group (House of Lords Ruling 1985). The 'mature enough to understand' principle has been subject to debate in all health matters. New laws have clarified that parents have 'duties and obligations to children, not rights over them'. This has allowed more leeway in decisions on treatment of those aged under 16 years and on whether young people may be seen alone by a doctor.

Evidence suggests that teenagers who become pregnant are less likely to complete school, get qualifications or have a job. This may lead to financial disadvantage, deprivation and social isolation. Those with lower educational success are more likely to smoke, to indulge in early sexual experience and more likely to drink excessively. In other words those with the least hope for their own future may be more fatalistic about their own future. They may be less likely to seek advice, although they are the ones who are most likely to be at risk. It is also suggested that family functioning may be an important determinant in young people's health. They report that those with higher levels of family conflict were more likely to experience low self-esteem and were more likely to smoke.

Those working with adolescents therefore have a vital role to play in helping them achieve a better standard of health which in turn means a better quality of life.

Research

Bob Broad and Lesley Saunders of De Montfort University have published the results of a health survey entitled *The Health Needs of Young People Leaving Care* in collaboration with The Royal Philanthropic Society and East Surrey Health Authority, 1997. The following is a brief summary of the results of interviews with 48 young people. These interviews were undertaken by young care leavers themselves who were trained and paid to carry out the work. The author's comments are also included in italics.

Physical health
Measures to improve physical health, i.e. eating, exercise and living more healthily were low on young people's priorities, compared with trying to survive on minimum financial support, maintaining satisfactory social relationships, and getting on with their life – *young people experiencing life away from home, at college, university or on a training scheme may have similar dilemmas unless early health education is received.*

→

Being in care

For the majority the effects of being in care were alarming. This created stress and insecurity and prompted various responses including drug taking, depression, and ill health. Because these young people had had many placements, forming effective social, educational and emotional networks was difficult. A lack of understanding at school about their situation and low expectations of teachers made things worse – *young people who have had disordered lives in other ways may also be similarly affected.*

Choosing less healthy lifestyles to release stress

Young people felt that the immediate short-term emotional gain of not living as healthily as they might far outweighed their knowledge about the long-term consequences of an unhealthy lifestyle – *this could apply to adolescents and adults alike.*

Isolation and unhappiness

Isolation and unhappiness arose from:

- unsatisfactory accommodation
- sometimes living alone
- often with little money, work, or any support
- little hope of improvement.

– a recent study of young offenders in Wiltshire (The Oxford Study) highlighted similar feelings of despair whether the young person was living at home or was 'in care'.

Improving emotional support

The need for improving emotional support was seen as vital when young people are in care, preparing to leave, and after leaving care – *a traditional place for receiving emotional support in the past has been school and extended families. Many family members now work or live some way away. With the emphasis on examination results this school support has sadly declined.*

Professional attitudes

There was a relatively high proportion of young people with some form of mental illness. The young people felt that the attitude of the professionals especially regarding the provision of mental health services, was unhelpful – *the training of health professionals in communicating with, not only young people but also black and ethnic minority families, requires a high profile campaign for improvement.*

Professional relationships

Many young people lacked satisfactory personal relationships, so had high expectations from professionals. Consequently they felt disappointment if/when the standard of that relationship fell short of the mark. Past disappointments concerning relationships with social workers could also explain low expectations and not 'opening up' – *most professionals are very concerned that time constraints brought about by budget cutbacks prevent the development of better relationships with young people. There is obviously a need for prioritisation of time.*

Priorities in determining good health

One surprising result of the report was that four of the top five determinants of health identified by the young people are not generally considered to be health issues. Four of the bottom five would normally be considered to be health issues – *it would be interesting to compare the results if the same question was asked to a cross section of similarly aged young people in differing circumstances. However, what is important from this research is the need for inter-agency working. There should be constant reminders to avoid preconceived ideas of the health priorities of adolescents.*

These priorities should not have been a surprising conclusion considering the World Health Organisation's definition of health made nearly 50 years ago:

> *"Health is a state of complete mental, physical and emotional well-being and not merely the freedom from disease or infirmity."* (W.H.O.)

The table below clearly shows that a great deal of re-thinking needs to be done to re-appraise the whole question of adolescent health. Maybe the health message is not getting across to young people because it is the wrong message that is being given.

Results when interviewees were asked to identify and prioritise the five most important things in determining their own health

Theme	In top 5 priorities	Top priority
Feelings about life	70.8	15.4
Housing	60.4	20.5
Close personal relationships	56.3	17.9
Care experience	41.7	12.8
Depression	41.7	12.8
Employment	37.5	2.6
Using drugs/solvents	29.2	10.3
Leisure	27.1	2.6
Experience of leaving care	27.1	2.6
Relaxation	25.0	2.6
Mental health services	22.9	5.1
Education and training	20.8	0.0
Eating habits	16.7	2.6
Physical health services	16.7	0.0
Smoking	8.3	0.0
Drinking	6.3	0.0

Using the health service

Many teenagers need to know:
- how to make an appointment
- how to sign on at a G.P. surgery
- how to access a G.P. when away from home
- that most emergencies can be dealt with by a doctor avoiding the need for a 999 call

- what entitlement they have to advice, check-ups, medicines, contraception or an abortion
- what their rights/expectations should be if they go into hospital.

Procedures and practices vary within health authorities so it is important to know what happens in individual areas and what a G.P. surgery has to offer.

When a young person is seen by a doctor for the first time they may be embarrassed, shy or unable to share their problem. Accompanying them to the surgery may help, so might talking about the problem beforehand or offering to join them initially and then leaving the consultation room when appropriate. Simon, a normally well behaved 16 year old, had recently become quite disruptive and a cause for concern for his teacher. Eventually, in confidence, he admitted to his teacher that he had lumps on his testicles and thought he might have cancer or HIV or AIDS. He didn't feel he could tell his parents so the teacher allowed him to use the office telephone to make an appointment at the doctor. She also went along to the surgery with him, but not into the consulting room. The prognosis was good, Simon's behaviour improved and the teacher/pupil relationship was enhanced.

Medical details/records

It is a good idea for all young people to keep their own medical records which might include:

- Name
- National Health Number
- Blood pressure
- Height and weight
- Immunisations (incl. dates):
  - measles
  - rubella
  - MMR (measles, mumps and rubella)
  - polio
  - tetanus

→

- Doctor's name, telephone number and address
- Dentist's name, telephone number and address
- Dates for future:
  - boosters
  - medical/dental/hospital check-ups/treatments
- Blood group
- Other specific details
  - past medical history
  - family medical history

Some young people exhibit apparent medical symptoms or admit to having a particular ailment when in fact it is a cry for help or a need to have someone to listen to them.

Health problems

In *Health of Adolescents in Primary Care* (Royal College of General Practitioners) it is suggested that young people should know the following so they are able to start taking responsibility for their own health:

Headaches

Everyone gets headaches from time to time. If you develop a very severe headache or it is associated with a high fever, a stiff neck or a rash, it could be meningitis, so contact a doctor quickly.

Coughs, colds and flu-like illnesses

Most of these are caused by viruses and cannot be treated by antibiotics. There are, however, a number of things you can do to relieve the unpleasant symptoms of:

- sore throat	- headache
- aching limbs	- fevers

Take lots of fluids and soluble aspirin or paracetamol. Gargling helps a very sore throat. You will usually begin to get better after a few days. If it does not settle, or you begin to feel worse, you can contact the school/college nurse or a doctor.

If you have a sore throat which lasts longer than expected, it is possible that you have glandular fever. There is a blood test available to check the diagnosis. Usually there is no specific treatment and the advice is much the same as for other viruses.

Meningitis symptoms

The germs that cause bacterial meningitis are present in some 15% of people's throats and are spread between people by coughing, sneezing or kissing, but they cannot live outside the body for long. The germs cannot be picked up from water supplies, swimming pools, building or factories.

Everyone should be aware of the early symptoms of meningitis, and should seek immediate medical advice if they have some of the following symptoms:

– headache	– dislike of bright lights
– temperature/fever	– drowsiness/lethargy
– vomiting	– joint pains
– neck stiffness	
– a rash of red/purple spots which look like bruising under the skin.	

Early diagnosis and treatment greatly increase the chances of a full recovery.

Diarrhoea and vomiting

This can be unpleasant but does not usually last long. If you are being sick, take small regular sips of water – you will absorb some and it helps stop dehydration. Hot water bottles help relieve stomach ache. Vomiting usually stops within a few hours. Diarrhoea can last longer. This is helped by not eating but drinking lots of clear fluids for 24 hours. Avoid milk during this time. If you have just come back from foreign places it is worth getting a doctor's advice.

Health professionals

It is a good idea to invite health professionals into schools/colleges/youth clubs/children's homes. However, it is important to ensure that whoever comes must:

- be prepared
- know what to expect in terms of time, space, facilities
- be willing to answer questions, often explicit and to not show embarrassment
- understand adolescence and adolescent behaviour. Their attitude should not be influenced by others
- be prepared to talk to the young people without them being supervised by others
- have a plan in place in case things go wrong.

Some topics which might be covered in discussion either by the health professionals or by those working directly with the young people are:

– alcohol: consumption and abuse	– acne
– HIV and AIDS	– contraception
– diet	– abortion
– nutrition	– puberty
– eating disorders	– period pains
– ethnic and cultural health differences	– depression
– drug taking	– diabetes
– cancer prevention: cervical/skin/lung	– disability
– asthma	– reducing accidents
– suicide prevention	– exercise
– smoking	– sports injury prevention

Positive approaches to health care

There are many excellent leaflets available from G.P. surgeries, health clinics or health promotion centres. However, sometimes these are couched in negative terms. The following are examples of positive approaches to health which could act as guides for work in some of the areas mentioned above.

Contraception

If you use contraception to prevent getting yourself or your girlfriend pregnant, you will be:

- free to make choices in your life
- free to enjoy your teenage years without responsibilities
- able to go where and when you please
- able to live with whom you wish
- not be beholden to anyone
- able to have children when *you* and *your* partner want and are ready
- given time to learn about relationships
- in a position to decide with whom you would like to have a child
- be able to say yes or no to sex which will give you confidence and freedom.

Smoking

What happens when you give up cigarettes?

- **Within 20 minutes** your blood pressure drops, your pulse rate drops to normal, the temperature of your hands and feet increases to normal.
- **After 8 hours** – the carbon monoxide level in your blood drops to normal, the oxygen level in your blood increases to normal.
- **After 24 hours** – the chances of having a heart attack decrease.
- **After 48 hours** – your nerve ends start regrowing, your ability to smell and to taste things improves.
- **After 72 hours** – your bronchial tubes begin to relax, your breathing becomes easier, your lung capacity increases.
- **After 2 weeks to 3 months** – your circulation improves, your lung functions are improved.
- **After 1 to 9 months** – coughing, sinus congestion, tiredness, shortness of breath, all improve, the linings of your lungs regrow normally, your overall energy is improved.

- **After 5 years** – risk of death from lung cancer for the average smoker decreases from 137 per 100,000 people to 72, and after 10 years to 12 (which is almost the rate for non-smokers).
- **After 10 years** – all pre-cancerous cells have been replaced, risk of other cancers such as those of the mouth, throat, bladder, kidney and cervix is decreased as well.

Conclusion

A school in Glasgow, in collaboration with the local leisure centre, has introduced a scheme to encourage both healthy eating and exercise. This is a positive way of encouraging young people to eat healthily as they then get discounts or free use of leisure facilities. This type of scheme could easily be adapted for other areas of health.

One's own health is a personal matter so if young people are given plenty of positive information on a wide variety of health related subjects they will be better able and will want to make healthy decisions that affect their lives.

Chapter 10

Promoting equality

How would you feel if your own child was being described in a derogatory way? How would you feel if you were the only black student in your class? How would you feel if you were blind and walked into a room knowing everyone could see you but you couldn't see them – angry? shy? embarrassed? As individuals it is often not possible to change other people's behaviour or certain situations. However, by providing information and knowledge to young people it will help them to learn how to cope with their situation. It should also be possible by using open discussion, scenarios and direct situational work with young people, to heighten their awareness, understanding and tolerance.

The following principles form the basis for this chapter:
- promotion of anti-discriminatory practice
- maintenance of confidentiality of individuals
- promotion and support of individual rights and choice
- acknowledgement of individuals' personal beliefs and identity
- supporting individuals through effective communication.

The Council for Racial Equality gives the following definitions of discrimination:
- **Direct discrimination** happens when someone is treated worse than others or segregated from them because of their race, colour, nationality, ethnic or national origins.
- **Indirect discrimination** happens when everyone seems to be treated in the same way but, in practice, people from a certain ethnic group are put at a greater disadvantage.
- **Victimisation** – if someone is victimised because they have complained about discrimination, or because they have supported someone else's complaint, this, too, is unlawful discrimination.

The definition of disability as noted in *Disabled People in Britain and Discrimination. A Case for Anti-Discrimination Legislation*, p.2 1991 by Colin Barnes is:

> **"Impairment** *is the functional limitation within the individual caused by physical, mental or sensory impairment.*
>
> **Disability** *is the loss or limitation of opportunities to take part in the mainstream of the community on an equal level with others due to physical and social barriers."*

Social services, health, voluntary organisations, parents and other interested bodies including schools should work in partnership with the young person.

Some disabilities inhibit natural maturity and may delay learning processes. This must be taken into account in preparing young people for leaving care and providing after care, including liaising with other agencies if they are looked after by the local authority.

The Children Act 1989 defines a category of children **in need** for whom social services departments should provide services, if necessary, to safeguard and promote their welfare. A child is defined by the Act as being **in need** if:

- they are unlikely to achieve or maintain, or to have the opportunity of achieving or maintaining, a reasonable standard of health or development without the provision of services by a local authority under this Part (of the Act)
- their health or development is likely to be significantly impaired, or further impaired, without the provision of such services
- they are disabled.

'Development' means physical, intellectual, emotional, social or behavioural development and 'health' means physical or mental health.

The Children Act (Scotland) 1995 and The Children (Northern Ireland) Order 1995 make similar definitions.

Social Services must also develop clear assessment procedures within agreed criteria which take account of the child's and family's needs and preferences, racial and ethnic origins, their culture, religion and any special needs relating to the circumstances of individual families.

When a young person leaves school there are a variety of provisions which must be taken into consideration including welfare, health, education and employment.

Working with young people with disabilities

Many young people experience some form of impairment but this can range from a minor condition such as myopia to a major dysfunction such as paraplegia; moreover the extent to which an impairment disables a young person and the extent to which such a disability is perceived as a handicap will vary enormously and be dependent upon a large number of extraneous factors – adapted from *Looking After Children, Research into Practice.*

It is vitally important to remember that young people with disabilities are young people first; they have the same physical, sexual, emotional and social needs as anyone else. The way that these needs are fulfilled may not necessarily be quite the same as for able bodied young people.

People use different terms to suit the occasion or sometimes to prevent embarrassment, often to themselves. A politically correct organisation that was funding a recent book insisted on the term 'with disabilities' being used whereas a critical reader who was black and disabled and proud of the description she had chosen for herself, felt the word 'disabled' should be used throughout the book.

Terms to Avoid	Use
victim of	person who has/person with/person who experienced
crippled by	person who has/person with
suffering from	person who has/person with
afflicted by	person who has/person with
wheelchair bound	wheelchair user
invalid (means not valid)	disabled person
mental	disabled person

Offensive	Preferred
handicap	disability
handicapped person	disabled person
spastic	cerebral palsy
deaf and dumb, deaf/mute	deaf or partial hearing
Mongoloid	Downs syndrome
cripple, crippled	disabled person or mobility impaired
the blind	blind person, partially sighted
the deaf	deaf people
mentally handicapped, backward, dull	learning difficulty
retarded, idiot, imbecile	developmental disability
mute, dummy	speech difficulty
crazy, maniac, insane	emotional disability
abnormal	exceptional, different

When working with all young people, but particularly disabled young people, emphasise the uniqueness and worth rather than individual differences. Efforts can do much to eliminate the 'them' and 'us' attitude that hampers the integration of disabled young people. It is also important to remember disabled people come from all communities, they may also be black and/or gay. The whole person should be considered, their culture and community, likes and dislikes. Consult them in any planning for their time with you and for their future.

Disability should not be negated or denied. Disabled young people may need help in understanding and accepting the idea that they should be proud of themselves and of their difference. Help may be needed to combat some of the barriers in our society such as:

The environment
- public transport
- housing
- public buildings
- roads

- walkways
- leisure centres
- day centres
- access to information

Attitudes – the general public often think the disabled are:
- incapable
- in need of special/separate provision
- brave
- courageous
- tragic

- bitter
- have a chip on their shoulder
- disability = low intelligence
- cheerful in the face of adversity

Disabled young people are rarely portrayed as part of mainstream culture – not in soaps or game shows. Documentaries on disability often pull at the heart strings and charity advertising is condescending. Disabled people sometimes seem to be shown as unemployable, invisible and the only important thing is to find a cure. Institutions are all equally guilty at times – the education system; medical institutions; legal systems; social services department; the family; class system.

By open discussion with others, barriers can be broken down and greater awareness and understanding developed which hopefully will enable all young people to live and work alongside each other.

"I haven't been given the same chances as someone who has not got a learning disability and I think it is unfair the way people with learning disabilities are treated." – Neil Armstrong in *Children in Focus*, Summer 1995, The Children's Society.

It is generally accepted that children with special educational needs should be placed in ordinary schools wherever possible. All children should have equal access to education, and disabled children should be able to receive education *"in a manner conducive to the fullest possible social integration and individual development"*. Sadly all too often education authorities find a way round this using the excuse that they are looking to harness an 'efficient use of resources'.

Advocacy in Action (1992) states that *"Disabled people and other 'user groups' have to learn how to represent their own views effectively and make realistic choices. This requires a huge range of skills around confidence, empowerment, information exchange, decision-making and negotiation."*

Professionals and policy makers have training needs around power-sharing, good communication, civil rights and equality. How important then is it for disabled young people to learn these skills and for everyone to work together to ensure a better quality of life for disabled young people?

Practical suggestions for working with disabled young people

The following are a few tips disabled people have suggested which should help in achieving success for young people:

- Do offer help, but don't get upset if it is rejected – sometimes it will be welcome, but sometimes it won't be needed or may hinder the disabled person doing it in their own, possibly slower but effective way.

- Young people particularly may become angry or aggressive as they try to come to terms with or want to learn to become independent.

- Do not make assumptions – many people have invisible disabilities such as epilepsy.

- Don't make comments like *'I don't know how you manage'* or *'I'd die if I was blind/deaf/couldn't walk'*.

- Speak directly to the person, not to whoever may be with them. People still say *'Does he take sugar?'*

- Obtain as much knowledge regarding the young person's special needs/disability as soon as possible.

- Have high but realistic expectations.

- Stress the good things.

- Praise, reassure.
- Encourage the young person to take part in a wide variety of activities.
- Help/teach them to play, find activities they can do individually, with groups in similar situations, with all young people.
- Help the young person to mix with others.
- Help them become as independent as possible.
- Don't treat them differently but as individuals.
- Talk to them, discuss, explain.
- Sometimes young people with disabilities need firm boundaries. Set them.
- Be patient.

Wheelchair users

- Don't lean on wheelchairs. The chair is part of someone's body space and it is extremely annoying.
- Do not grab the back of someone's wheelchair to push them along. Always ask first if help is required and do not be offended if it is refused.
- Never grab a person's wheelchair when they are manoeuvring it; such well meant help is dangerous and may hurt the disabled person's arm or wrists.
- If you have to negotiate a chair up or down steps, get the advice of the wheelchair user on how best to do it.
- Try to seat or situate yourself at eye level with the person as much as possible. It is extremely difficult to join in and hear conversations which are going on over your head. Try not to stand too near, causing the wheelchair user to have to crane the neck to keep eye contact.
- Reserve head patting for animals even though a wheelchair user's head may be temptingly at the same height. Disabled people find this sign of affection patronising and inappropriate.

Young people with speech impairments

- Wait and do not jump in to finish what you think they might be going on to say.

- Don't pretend to understand if you don't. Ask the person to say it again, and repeat what you understand to gain confirmation.
- If they have a facilitator, use that person **only** as an interpreter, i.e. do not engage in conversation directly with the facilitator.

Meeting/communicating with deaf young people

- Don't talk with something in your mouth such as a pen or a sweet and try to remember to keep your hand away from your mouth.
- Do not stand against a window or bright light; it hinders lip reading. Stand where your face is best lit.
- Don't talk away from the deaf person, e.g. to a blackboard or other people.
- Don't use sign language unless you know the deaf person uses it. Deaf people often choose not to use sign language, so provide interpreters for meetings, interviews etc..
- If you are not understood by the deaf person rephrase a sentence, keeping it brief. Repeat or rephrase a whole sentence not just a single word. If you don't understand, don't pretend that you do.
- If you are with a deaf person when some audible warning, or announcement is made, say what is happening, e.g. a fire alarm.

Working with blind young people

- Don't be afraid to offer help, but speak first and ask the young person if they want assistance. Don't be upset if they say they don't need help.
- If guiding a blind person, go first, i.e. slightly ahead of them, with their arm resting on yours. Get into trains, buses before them, and if entering a car, guide their hand to the roof over the car door.
- Give verbal warnings, say when you are approaching steps and whether these go up or down, and if helping a blind person into a car, say which way it is facing. Guess and say the distance if you can.
- Indoors, describe furniture as you move past it and mention head level hazards. To help someone to a chair, guide their arm to the back or armrest so that they can seat themselves.
- Do not leave doors half open.

- Meals – say what the food is before it is served. Don't fill cups, glasses to the brim.

- When talking to a blind person always introduce yourself and the people with you including their relative positions to you. It may help to go over to them and touch them on the arm as you first speak.

- If in a group, say the name of the other people to whom you are speaking or get them to introduce or announce themselves so that the blind person can keep track of the conversation.

Working with black and ethnic minority young people

Thirteen practitioners, the majority of whom are from minority ethnic groups in their country, have joined together to produce *Anti-Racist Work with Young People, European Experiences and Approaches,* Russell House Publishing 1997. All the authors have been on the receiving end of racism so are able to bring to the book both personal and professional experiences. The book provides case material and activities for work with young people as well as a sound theoretical base so it is not proposed to reproduce similar material here, more to give some examples and suggestions.

One area of concern both for these authors and for many others working in the field of anti-racist practice is communication. The Cantel School in Southampton produced a handout for teachers which has now been developed as a general guide.

Another very useful book is *Religion, Ethnicity, Sex Education, Exploring the Issues,* compiled and edited by Rachel Thomson on behalf of the Sex Education Forum published by the National Children's Bureau which highlights the importance of understanding different cultural norms such as those regarding puberty, circumcision etc..

In attempting not to appear racist or to encourage young people to maintain their cultural identity it is possible to forget that the young people's views are paramount. The following are two real examples:

Aysha was 15 and the second eldest in a Muslim family of four girls. During discussions at school Aysha always seemed very knowledgeable about sexual

The 'Do's'

- refer to influential and famous people from a variety of cultures
- value and celebrate examples of work from various cultures
- offer alternative explanations and opinions
- explain why certain phrases, words and language are inappropriate or unacceptable
- encourage all young people to help with language understanding
- celebrate individual experiences, backgrounds and lifestyles
- ensure that vocabulary is relevant to the young person's culture and religion
- encourage young people to see one another as equal and different
- show an awareness of the timing of festivals and holy days
- make ground rules for behaviour absolutely clear
- appreciate that Asian extended wedding celebrations are a cultural norm and not an excuse for a good time
- alert others of any inter-ethnic factions
- ask young people how to pronounce or spell their names
- refer to names as 'first' rather than Christian names
- feel comfortable in using the word 'Black' as a positive noun
- remember that during Ramadan certain allowances may have to be made to allow young people to fast
- seek advice about such things as meat and alcohol, the use of which is sometimes forbidden in some religions and life styles.

The 'Don'ts'

- refer to anyone as coloured – Black/Asian is acceptable – positive words
- call people only by the name 'Singh' or 'Kaur' – these are religious titles
- take offence if Asian students refuse to look you in the eye when being reprimanded; lowering the eyes indicates humility/sorrow
- call Asians 'Indians' – most Asians are not from India
- take offence if West Indian girls giggle or grin initially when reprimanded – it may signify embarrassment
- insist on making some young people sit next to each other
- ban use of mother tongue, unless it undermines your authority or has a negative effect on the group
- ignore any written or oral, racially offensive comments
- use the word 'topknot' – Turban and Joora are correct
- use exclusively European (and male) names on documents; reflect the make-up of the community

matters, often more so than many of her contempories. Her teacher knew that, along with her sisters, she lived a very sheltered life and was puzzled by Aysha's knowledge especially as her parents were very strict. Eventually the teacher discovered that the girls were hiring explicit videos unknown to their parents as they felt they wanted to know more about life in order to make up their own minds on sexual matters. In other words it was their choice and any attempt to persuade them to follow the strict Muslim ways of their family was not appropriate.

Kulie was very keen on basketball and desperately wanted a pair of trainers similar to those worn by the rest of his team. He wanted to spend his special needs allowance on these trainers. His carer in the children's home felt that what he should have was a set of tapes of his native language Punjabi which she bought for him. He was also encouraged to eat food appropriate to his religion. Kulie was not only very angry that he was not consulted, he gave up playing basketball because he said he was too embarrassed to wear his existing trainers. He also said that his family had never brought him up to follow any religion and if in the future he wanted to learn Punjabi or eat specific food he would, but at present he had no intention of so doing.

Observations/hints that may also be useful are:

- find out what the young people know about their family, culture and religion
- what would they like to know – help them discover this for themselves or together
- don't assume because they come from say, Bangladesh that, they are Muslim
- different people within different cultures and/or religions will have different attitudes and behaviour patterns so find out what is the norm for each young person, which may be completely different from the last teenager of that religion with whom you worked.
- what does the young person believe?
- what do they want to know?
- if you can't help where can they go for help?

Sex, sexuality and young people

People have sex for a variety of reasons including:

– excitement	– to feel attractive, wanted or loved
– habit	– out of boredom or curiosity
– duty	– for power
– procreation	– influence
– lust	– manipulation
– peer pressure	– abuse
– to express love	– to dominate
– to please	– to frighten other people
– to relax	– to inflict pain
– to distract	

One young girl explained that during sex was the only time she was held, hugged or felt loved – a powerful motivator indeed at the time but what of the subsequent hurt and pain – an important pointer for those working with young people.

Most people receive some sex education during their lives, usually at school, which often focuses on the practical issues and rarely touches on attitudes or feelings. Young people who miss out on school often miss out on sex education altogether and have to rely on others for what is often mis-information. Alternatively they may pretend to know a good deal about sex rather than admit ignorance.

Many young people are sexually active from a young age. Many do not see themselves to be at risk of HIV. Many lack the necessary information, confidence, skills and self-esteem to avoid having sex when they don't want it or to negotiate safer sex. The aim of this section then is not to attempt to provide masses of information for those working with young people but to help them to feel able to discuss sex and sexuality openly and to help give young people the confidence to say 'no' if they so choose. Detailed leaflets on various specific areas are already available and some telephone numbers for contacts are in Appendix 1.

The Royal College of Obstetricians and Gynaecologists' report in 1991 stated:

> *"Sexuality is fundamental to individuals' happiness and a major factor in the stability of relationships between couples. Much of the difficulty that couples have in managing their sexual activity is due to their feeling that sex is embarrassing, disapproved of and potentially dangerous, with the result that sexual pleasure is mixed with guilt and anxiety. Young people may know about the biology of sex (intercourse and reproduction) but have rarely been given the vocabulary and the skills they need to communicate with each other about this aspect of life (sexuality, sexual activity and relationships). This is a consequence of frequent inability of their parents or teachers to communicate with them openly about sex and the aura of anxiety and criticism that many other people show when talking with young people about sex.*
>
> *As a result, young women have difficulty in accepting their sexuality and young people have difficulty in communicating verbally with each other. Consequently intercourse tends to occur ... without planning and often without adequate contraception."*

Sex is not just about genital contact. It has physical, mental, emotional, individual, social, cultural, religious and political dimensions. Anyone working with young people must come to terms with their own feelings, beliefs and uncertainties before they will be able to openly discuss sex and sexuality with adolescents. The chart on p.147 may be helpful in giving some starting points for discussion.

Young people can best be helped when they can learn to say yes or no to sexual relationships and to choose the kind of sex they want. Helping young people to understand, know what they want and to be involved in these decisions will help them take control over their lives. Disabled young people have similar sexual desires and additionally they should be assisted in order to be able to express their sexuality in the ways they wish.

Often those working with young people are hampered by the lack of clear policies and guidelines on this subject. They are not sure how far they can go in addressing issues of sexuality with young people or are not equipped to deal with differing situations such as:

- very sexually active young people (they might have been sexually abused)

Sexuality					
Sexual practice	**Sexual orientation**	**Sensuality**	**Social structures**	**Political dimensions**	**Institutional oppressions**
including celibacy	heterosexual lesbian gay bisexual attraction and desire	food sharing meals candle light clothing fabrics exercise touch massage nature elements – wind, sun, water, earth, heat, cool, ice aromas, oils intimacy sharing secrets dreams fantasy dance art music	marriage living together wedding rings conditioning gender stereotypes dress and grooming rites of passage etc. circumcision bar mitzvah retreats first menstruation tampons sexual experience sex education dating going steady engagement	feminism women's groups lesbian and gay groups – demonstrations celebrations mothers and toddlers groups black groups elders groups	oppressions, incl. sexism, racism, heterosexism, ableism, ageism, class etc. institutionalised legal system age of consent medical system mental health equal opportunity programmes

From Sexuality, *Young People and Care*, CCETSW 1993, Russell House Publishing 1994

- young girls obsessed with older men
- inferiority complex about the size of their body parts.

As this is often a controversial area they tend to err on the side of caution by not raising questions. Even when clear guidelines are available, it is important that one's own inhibitions and beliefs are examined and addressed, for example the Catholic social worker who disapproves of contraception or the Pro-life worker who is against abortion or the teacher who is not sure of her own sexuality.

Sex can mean different things to different people. It is important to check out meanings in order to avoid misunderstandings. For instance, if a young person expresses concern about HIV because they have had sex, it might be assumed they mean penetrative sex. However, it could just mean masturbation, kissing, heavy petting, foreplay, ejaculation. Delicate questioning is required but it may turn out to be the opportunity needed to discuss much broader issues of sex and sexuality.

Other issues that need to be addressed or borne in mind, when working on issues of sexuality are:
- peer pressure
- confusion
- not feeling at risk
- experimentation – 'to taste hidden fruits'
- suspicion of adult motives
- relationships and intimacy
- cultural issues
- power and abuse
- drugs and alcohol
- pregnancy
- coercion – 'you must have sex to show your faithfulness or love'
- conflict and pressure.

Young people need an opportunity to:
- increase their self-awareness by exploring their feelings and attitudes to these matters
- develop confidence, self-esteem, communication and social skills.

Cultural and class issues also need to be addressed such as:

- different cultures may have different norms regarding arranged marriages
- age of marrying
- sex before marriage
- monogamy and polygamy
- rites of passage or initiation ceremonies
- gender role expectations
- women's and men's status or role in society and within relationships
- power
- modesty
- independence
- sexual behaviour
- homosexuality
- drug use
- male and female circumcision
- expectations about proving fertility or virility
- talking openly about sexuality
- use of contraception
- abortion

Gender

It is important that everyone has the opportunity to understand, to challenge and to decide for themselves their sexual role and identity. Gender stereotyping affects us in many ways such as in the area of sexuality and sex role conditioning. The feminist movement during the past 30 years has identified inequalities and differences and currently there is much debate on the gender issue and some backlash. The pop-star Lauren Laverne says *"Feminism is a positive word imbued with a lot of positive history. The basic idea of feminism is equality to men"* whereas Louise Wener, another singer, refuses to call herself a feminist *"There's so much about traditional feminist thought that annoys me"*

Young lesbian women and gay men

At least ten per cent of the population are not heterosexual yet for many the idea of lesbian and gay sexuality being as valid as heterosexuality is difficult to accept. Gay clubs and the gay scene have become an every day part of life and the term gay refers to both lesbians and gays. For the remainder of this chapter the term gay will be so used as it is often the preferred term of both groups.

Some common misconceptions:
- lesbian or gay sexuality is the same as paedophilia
- all sex abuse is carried out by gays
- 'they're not really gay, it's just a passing phase'
- 'they've become gay because of the crowd they go around with'
- all gays have HIV or AIDS

It is important for anyone working with young people regardless of circumstance to:
- have accurate information about lesbian and gay sexuality
- be able to dispel the myths with facts

Women who have sex with women and men who have sex with men may not identify as lesbian or gay. This is a western concept. Many such individuals may be married. In any culture, it is important not to assume that people will only be attracted to the opposite gender. This will be especially important in working with members of minority cultures who may feel strong pressure to hide their preference. If in discussing sexual matters an interpreter is required, professional interpreters should be used to avoid embarrassment which might be caused if informal interpreters such as family, friends or community leaders are used.

Young people with same-sex attraction should be supported and an adult who is told by a young person about their sexuality should realise that it means they see the adult as trustworthy. The adult needs to be able to empower the young person to be sexual in a way that is safe and healthy for them. However there are certain legal considerations in working with young people on issues of sex and sexuality which may need to be confirmed and highlighted.

The debate about the age of consent for gays is ongoing and the current legislation in England and Wales is noted under the legal chapter, p.163, but it is anticipated that this may be reduced in the future to 16 years for all forms of sexual activity. However it is important that young people have the law explained to them.

One area of concern is the lack of clubs for young gays. These young people end up coming on to the commercial gay scene and going to bars at quite a young age forcing them to grow up a lot quicker and before they may be ready.

Some groups of young people will readily want to discuss sex and sexuality and will instigate a debate at every opportunity, others will need help and confidence boosting before opening up. In all cases, however, care must be taken to avoid embarrassment to some young people, to challenge stereotyping and inaccurate facts and to ensure everyone has an opportunity to speak either during the debate or later privately.

As well as discussions, there are now some very good videos on specific subjects, books, posters and board games. What is important is that the information given to young people should be:

- non judgmental
- factually correct
- non-prejudiced
- given discreetly and with respect.

Chapter 11

Young people's rights and the law

Young people are often very keen to know their rights. Rights without responsibilities are useless.

This Chapter briefly summarises some of the more common laws that might affect adolescents. The Children's Legal Centre produce an easy to use pamphlet called *At what age can I?* which may also be useful. This booklet also highlights the many inconsistencies in British law. For instance a young person may have sex and marry with parental consent at 16 but cannot vote until they are 18; they can work in a mine at 16 but not get a tattoo until they are 18 years old.

The present government in the UK is considering raising the age limit to 18 years for buying tobacco and for having sex with someone in authority such as a teacher or a care worker. Conversely, in order to fall into line with the ruling from the European Court of Human Rights, it is anticipated that the age of consent for gay sex will become 16 for all.

Many people have suggested that there should be a minister with responsibility for the interests of children and young people. Others would go further and set up groups around the country to listen to the views of young people to ensure their voice is heard in parliament.

The notes in this chapter could be used purely as a reference following a request for information but they could also be helpful as a starting point for conversation either generally or to discuss a particular incident or behaviour pattern. For ease of use they have been produced in alphabetical order.

Adoption
When parent(s) are unable to, have died or do not wish to care for the young person, then the young person may be adopted and the adoptive

parents will automatically be given parental responsibility. Many checks are carried out and the young person is consulted throughout the process and must agree to the adoption. Quite often the young person will not see birth parent(s) unless it is an open adoption which means access via letters, telephone calls and sometimes visits have been agreed at the time of the adoption.

Advocacy

Advocacy is the activity of achieving rights for children, whether through the process of acting on their behalf, or of assisting them to act for themselves. Anyone may be an advocate. Some local authorities who employ people to act as advocates on behalf of young people stipulate certain relevant qualifications/experience.

The two approaches to advocacy are **active** and **passive**.

Active is giving young people the power to take any action themselves.

Passive is primarily about protecting the welfare of young people, in terms of their entitlement to equal status in, and consideration by, society.

Alcohol

Young people aged between 5 and 16 may drink alcohol on private premises under the care and control of an adult. Anyone may enter licensed premises but to go into a bar alone a young person must be 14. No one may buy alcohol or drink alcohol in a bar until the age of 18. In a licensed restaurant at 16 a young person may buy and drink beer, porter, cider or perry with a meal. Someone aged 18 or over may purchase wine which anyone under 18 may drink whilst in the restaurant.

Benefits

There are numerous benefits available but as the entitlement for these changes from time to time specific information is not provided. However, leaflets are available from the various benefit offices, some post offices and libraries and also Citizens Advice Bureaux.

Changing names

Anyone may change their name simply by asking other people to call them by any name they wish. If they wish to do this legally, they can use a deed poll or statutory declaration but they must have written permission from whoever has parental responsibility for them or permission from the court.

Children Act 1989; Children (Scotland) Act 1995; Children (Northern Ireland) Order 1995

The main thrust of these Acts is that the wishes and feelings of the child must be taken into consideration providing the child is able to understand what is going on. What this means in practice is that from the age of about 10 or 11 young people should routinely be consulted about decisions that affect their lives. Except in exceptional circumstances parents should also be involved in this decision making even when the young person does not live at home.

Sometimes court orders have to be made but only if it is in the best interests of the child. These orders automatically stop when a young person is 18 if not before but he or she may apply to the court earlier to rescind the order if appropriate. Court orders are only made if a better way to help the young person cannot be found.

Child Assessment Order – is made where the parent(s) have refused to co-operate or the local authority thinks the young person might be in danger of significant harm but is in no immediate danger at present. The order requires the young person to be taken to a specified place for assessment.

Emergency Protection Order (Exclusion Order in Scotland) – is made if the court has reason to believe that the young person will come to or is suffering from significant harm.

Care Order and Interim Care Order – are made to protect and help the young person and gives the local authority parental responsibility jointly with the parent(s) whom the young person should be encouraged to see. The Children (Scotland) Act 1995 provides a different range of orders but the overriding principles are similar.

Contact Order – states that the person with whom the young person lives must allow the young person to stay with, visit, write to or telephone anyone mentioned in the order.

Supervision Order (usually lasts up to 1 year but no longer than 3 years) and **Interim Supervision Order** (usually up to 8 weeks, sometimes extended a further 4 weeks) – is where the court appoints a supervisor, usually from social services, to advise, help and befriend a young person and to ensure any other conditions the court sets are carried out. The Children (Scotland) Act 1995 provides a different range of orders but the overriding principles are similar.

Residence Order – states with whom the child must live and usually lasts until the young person is 16 but occasionally 18 years.

Prohibited Steps Order (Interdict in Scotland) – states that certain things cannot happen without the court's permission and usually lasts until the young person is 16 years.

Specific Issue Order – is made where there is a disagreement about how the young person is to be brought up such as schooling, religion, health care, etc.. It means the court will decide, after consulting others, what should be done and how it should be done in the interests of the child. It usually ends when the young person is 16.

Discrimination

It is generally unlawful to discriminate against a person on the grounds of:
- colour
- race
- ethnic origin or nationality
- religion
- sex
- marital status
- disability

Discrimination at work, in schools and in the provision of services is unlawful.

Divorce

In response to pressure from children's organisations, certain procedures have been explicitly noted and the following should be taken into account:

"the wishes and feelings of the child in the light of his age and understanding and the circumstances in which those wishes were expressed; a requirement to have regard to the conduct of the parties in relation to the upbringing of the

child; the principle that, in the absence of evidence to the contrary, the welfare of the child will be best served by the child having regular contact with those who have parental responsibility for him and with other members of his family, and a requirement for the court to have regard to any risk to the child which may be attributable to actual or proposed arrangements for the child's future."

Driving

Minimum ages:

- At 16, young people who are provisional driving licence holders may drive motor tricycles, three wheeled cars or vans up to 500kg., invalid carriages, mowing machines, pedestrian controlled vehicles and mopeds.
- At 17 adolescents can also drive motorbikes with or without a sidecar, scooters, motor cars or light vans with up to nine seats/3500kg., all cars fitted with automatic transmission and agricultural tractors.
- At 18 teenagers can also drive small lorries between 3500 and 7500kg..
- At 21 anyone can also drive large lorries over 3500kg. with any number of axles, can tow a single axle trailer up to 5000kg. or any other trailer up to 750kg., small buses with between 9 and 16 passenger seats not used for hire or reward etc.

When learning to drive you must have someone supervising you who is over 21 years of age and has held a full driving licence for at least three years. If you do not comply with these requirements then it will result in a fine and penalty points or disqualification for the supervisor and possibly the learner driver as well. Once you have passed your test you must apply for your full driving licence within two years or you must take your test again.

Provisional motorcycle licences last for two years. If you do not pass your test within that time then you must wait another year to apply for a new provisional licence.

A written test must be passed before the driving test may be attempted.

Drugs – illegal

It is illegal to use, possess or supply certain drugs and in some circumstances simply to have them in the house is illegal. The police may search anyone, their house and their vehicles if they have reason to believe illegal drugs may be found.

Glue and other solvents are not illegal but a shopkeeper is committing an offence by selling them to a young person, knowing how they might be misused.

Education

Every local education authority has a duty to provide full-time free education for all children up to the age of 16 (from16-19 this duty is transferred to the Further Education Funding Council). It is the parent's/carer's duty to ensure the young person attends school. It is also the LEA's duty to ensure that young people with statements are educated where possible in mainstream schools.

Schools must provide a written statement about the school including the general principles regarding discipline.

Parents delegate to the school responsibility for the behaviour of young person. It is the parent's/carer's responsibility to ensure regular school attendance.

Teachers have a duty to *"take such care of the children in his charges as a careful parent would take of his own children"* and *"promote the general progress and well-being of individual pupils or classes or groups, maintain good order and discipline and safeguard the health and safety of pupils"*.

Local authorities have a duty to *"contribute towards the spiritual, moral, mental and physical development of the community ... to meet the needs of the population in their area"*.

Head teachers may exclude a young person from school providing they can justify the decision on the grounds of unreasonable behaviour by the young person. Local authorities and school governors must be informed. Appeals may be made by parents/carers. Local authorities may also re-instate the young person immediately or on a particular future date.

If a young person is out of school for any reason, school work should be provided. When a young person is in the last year of compulsory schooling they should receive careers advice and an opportunity to undertake work experience.

The Disability Discrimination Act 1995 requires added provision to be made for those with special needs.

Marriage

Young people aged 16-18 may only get married with the permission of both parents if they still live together or with permission from whoever has parental responsibility for them. It is illegal to get married if either person is already married or to marry a close relative such as a brother, sister, uncle or aunt (incest), but cousins may marry. To get married the person must be able to understand the ceremony and give consent. In Scotland young people over the age of 16 may marry without parental consent.

Meetings

Young people who are 'in care' should attend the meetings which must be held to plan for the young person's future (planning meetings and reviews). The following rights at a review were produced in *It's Your Meeting – A guide to help young people get the most from their review* (Ann Wheal and Ruth Sinclair, National Children's Bureau, 1995). However, the general principals are the same for all young people:

- you should be involved in deciding where and when the meeting takes place
- you should be listened to
- your wishes must be taken into account
- you may take someone with you to speak on your behalf if you wish
- you should know before the meeting what will be talked about at the meeting
- you may talk it over with someone you can trust before the meeting
- you can choose where you want to sit
- you can ask for your parents, carers or someone else to leave for some of the meeting
- you can have an interpreter if necessary or have other special facilities provided if you are disabled
- you can ask if you don't understand
- you should understand the decisions that are made and get a written copy

Money

Generally credit is not available until a young person is 18 years old unless they can provide guarantors who agree to take on the repayment of the loan if the young person ceases to pay.

Everyone, male and female, who becomes a parent is financially responsible for the child until they are 18 years old. The Child Support Agency is located in most D.S.S. offices and will advise on obtaining maintenance payments for any child.

Parental responsibility

If a father and mother are married to each other when the child is born or have since married, they both automatically have parental responsibility but if the parents did not get married only the mother automatically has parental responsibility. A father can:

- apply to the court for parental responsibility
- draw up a formal agreement with their mother which must be registered with the court; ask to be made a guardian
- be granted a residence order by the court.

Parental responsibilities last until a young person is 18 years old although these responsibilities diminish from the age of 16 years.

Parental responsibility means that the parents must ensure that a young person gets correct medical treatment, full education and that their physical, moral and religious needs are met. Parents also have the right to chastise their children reasonably.

The government in the UK is currently highlighting and emphasising the need for parental responsibility to be improved in areas such as school attendance, curfews and in the prevention of juvenile crime.

Police

The police can stop anyone in a public place if they suspect possession of prohibited articles such as offensive weapons, drugs or stolen goods but they can only search outer clothing such as coats, gloves etc. on the street. If a more intimate search is considered necessary the suspect will be taken to a police station.

If stopped or arrested the police should show their identity card and warrant if appropriate. Everyone is entitled to a copy of the search record which should be kept safely.

Anyone under 17 years must have a responsible adult present (parent, over 18 year old friend, social worker, teacher) during questioning. The police must inform the suspect why he or she has been arrested and explain their rights including access to a solicitor. Unless the offence is serious, release or charge must take place within 24 hours of detention.

A warrant is normally required to enter a private home unless police have reason to believe someone they wish to arrest is present; the search is linked directly to an arrest – they may wish to search before evidence can be removed; they are trying to stop or prevent serious violence or a breach of the peace.

Anyone under the age of 18 may appear in a Youth Court in England and Wales, over 18 the case will initially be heard in a Magistrates Court but may go to Crown Court for trial or sentencing. Social workers and probation officers are often asked for pre-sentence reports.

Sentences a young person might receive are:
- discharge
- binding over to keep the peace/behave well
- fine
- compensation order
- community service, supervision order, usually with conditions
- attendance centre order
- probation order
- combination order, which means supervision and community service
- curfew
- custody in young offender institution or secure accommodation depending upon age or seriousness of crime
- prison if over 16 years

A criminal record normally lasts between six months and three years depending upon the crime but for very serious offences such as murder the offender has a criminal record for ever.

The government has issued a white paper which the home secretary, Jack Straw has described as *"the most radical reform of the youth justice system since the second world war"*. This bill has the general approval of many interested parties although there is some resistance especially regarding the parenting order. The main points of the bill are:

- local curfew schemes to keep unsupervised under-10s off the streets after nine p.m.
- a parenting order aimed at mothers and fathers of young offenders requiring them to take responsibility for their children or face penalties
- a speedier justice system for persistent young offenders, aimed at drastically reducing the time between their arrest and punishment
- reparation orders to make young offenders face responsibility for their crimes. This could include apologising to the victim, cleaning graffiti, repairing criminal damage or writing a letter of apology
- wider powers to detain in secure accommodation those aged between 12 and 14
- the abolition of the rule of *doli incapax*, that presumes a child under 14 does not know the difference between right and wrong
- the formation of a youth justice board to co-ordinate the implication of punishment throughout England and Wales and to iron out the many existing anomalies among different parts of the country.

Records

Every young person has a right to see any records about them if they wish. There must be a very good reason for anyone refusing, but sometimes different agencies may think it is in the best interest of the young person not to see everything that has been written about them.

A child's birth must be registered within 42 days of the birth.

The Rights of the Child
The Rights of the Child (1923):

- The child must be protected beyond and above all considerations of race, nationality or creed.
- The child must be cared for with due respect for the family as an entity.

- The child must be given the means requisite for its normal development, materially, morally and spiritually.
- The child that is hungry must be fed, the child that is sick must be nursed, the child that is mentally or physically handicapped must be helped, the maladjusted child must be re-educated, the orphan and the waif must be sheltered and succoured.
- The child must be the first to receive relief in times of distress.
- The child must enjoy the full benefits provided by social welfare and social security schemes, must receive a training which will enable it, at the right time, to earn a livelihood, and must be protected against every form of exploitation.
- The child must be brought up in the consciousness that its talents must be devoted to the service of its fellow men.

1959 U.N. Declaration of the Rights of the Child
This declaration updated the 1923 version but added sections on freedom from discrimination. In some ways it was a response to the post war problems of refugees and genocide. It acknowledged the growing role of the state in terms of welfare provision and emphasised the need to protect children from discrimination. Because it was a declaration it was not a binding document in contrast to a convention which is.

1989 Convention on the Rights of the Child:
In this convention, children are defined as:

- Persons under the age of 18 years, or younger, according to national laws regarding the age of majority.

They are afforded rights of protection from:

- Abuse, exploitation, torture and armed conflicts.

Everyone is entitled to the right to life, to state care where necessary, to education, health services and social security. Families are identified as the best promoters of children's welfare. There is special mention of the needs of children with one or more disabilities, children who are being adopted, refugee children, children without families and children of minority groups. Children are perceived as citizens with rights to freedom of religion, of association, of privacy, and of access to information.

Sex and the law

It is illegal for any male to have sex with a female before she is 16, even if she agrees. Males (over the age of 10) can be prosecuted for unlawful sexual intercourse (rape). Sex between males is illegal for all men under 18. After 18, both partners must agree and the sexual act must be in private. Female homosexuality is not an offence; however, if either party is under 16 it can be classed as an indecent assault. As mentioned elsewhere, the age of consent for male homosexuals may shortly be reduced to 16 years.

Smoking

No one under the age of 16 may buy tobacco or smoke in public, but anyone at any age may smoke in private. Most local authorities and schools have their own rules about smoking on and off the premises. There is strong evidence that the legal age for purchasing tobacco is shortly to be increased to 18 and that smoking in public places will be banned.

Chapter 12

Conclusion

Evaluation and confirmation

There is a school of thought that says you should not be too understanding with adolescents and that they need someone or something against which to rebel. This may be true some of the time for some young people but equally it may be true that the rebellion is a sign of insecurity. Young people do not want, or like to be aggressive or antagonistic; they just do not have the skills to behave in any other way. Help them to acquire these skills so they may enjoy their life to the full.

In all work with young people it is important to evaluate what you are doing, why was it done that way, was there a better way? That is not to say that there is no place for spontaneity. The reverse. Many of the approaches in the book very easily become instinctive. However, it is important to stand back to evaluate in order to avoid complacency or missing important pointers. An example of this reflection is given by a foster carer when she heard from her other children that one adolescent did not want to attend an 18th birthday party where the whole family were attending. She had assumed he wanted to go to the party, but:

- he may be unhappy
- he doesn't want to answer questions
- doesn't know how to tell you he doesn't want to go
- it hasn't happened the way you expected
- he wants to go so much he may try too hard
- he needs genuine help in order to go, stay there and enjoy himself
- he has dynamics of his own
- he is uncertain what to expect.

This carer spoke to the lad and they talked about the options available to him by not going. Gradually it transpired that he really did want to go but was unsure what to expect and what was expected of him. The whole family went to the party which was the subject of conversation for many weeks to come.

Many things, of course, appear to go right both despite of, as well as because of well laid plans and discussion. After the event, talk it over, confirm that things were OK. Confirming is equally as important as evaluation, as a picture will emerge of what usually works and what does not work. Some people are afraid to say *"How did you see that working?"* (not *"How was that?"*).

Helping young people acquire analytical skills is worthwhile. To be able to evaluate and confirm when things go wrong and when there are successful outcomes will give confidence and reassurance for the future.

Young people's experiences, perceptions and understanding of life may not be what you think. You may be shocked; you may be saddened but equally you may be angry. Your own coping strategies for dealing with these emotions may be equally useful to pass on to the young people.

Appendix 1

Useful information

Alcohol
Alcoholics Anonymous
P.O. Box 1
Stonebow House
Stonebow
York YO1 2NJ
Tel: 01904 644026

Debt
National Debtline
318 Summer Lane
Birmingham B19 3RL
Tel: 0121 359 8501

Depression
The Samaritans
10 The Grove
Slough SL1 1QP
Tel: 01753 532713

Discriminination/Racism
The Commission for Racial Equality
Elliot House
10-12 Allington Street
London SW1E 5EH
Tel: 0171 828 7022

Disability
British Epilepsy Association
Anstey House
40 Hanover Square
Leeds LS3 1BE
Tel: 0113 243 9393
Free Phone 0800 309030

Scope
12 Park Crescent
London W1N 4EQ
Tel: 0171 636 5020

Drug Abuse
Release (Legal and Drugs Advice)
388 Old Street
London EC1V 9LT
Emergency Tel: 0171 603 8654
(24-hour emergency telephone
service)

Eating
Eating Disorders Association
1st Floor Wensum House
103 Prince of Wales Road
Norwich NR1 1DW
Tel: 01603 619090

Vegetarian Society
Parkdale, Dunham Road
Altringham
Cheshire WA14 4QG
Tel: 0161 928 0793

Health

British Heart Foundation
14 Fitzharding Street
London W1H 4DH
Tel: 0171 935 0185

Health Education Authority
Hamilton House
Mabledon Place
London WC1H 9TX
Tel: 0171 383 3833

Housing/Homelessness

Shelter
Housing Aid Information Team
88 Old Street
London EC1V 9HU
Tel: 0171 253 0202

Listening

The Samaritans
10 The Grove
Slough SL1 1QP
Tel: 01753 532713
0171 284 4793

Pregnancy/Contraception

Family Planning Association (UK)
2-12 Pentonville Road
London N1 9SP
Tel: 0171 837 5432

Solvent Abuse

Re-Solv
30A High Street
Stone
Staffordshire ST15 8AW
Tel: 01785 817885

Sex/Sexuality

Brook Advisory Centres
165 Grays Inn Road
London WC1X 8UD
Tel: 0171 713 9000

Avert
(an information service on
contraception etc.)
11-13 Denne Parade
Horsham
West Sussex RH12 1JD
Tel: 01403 210202

Lesbian and Gay Switchboard
Tel: 0171 837 7324

Smoking

Ash (Action on Smoking and
Health)
16 Fitzharding Street
London W1H 9PL
Tel: 0171 224 0743

Education

The High/Scope Institute
Coperfield House
190-192 Maple Road
Penge SE2 8HT
Tel: 0181 676 0220

The National Portage Association
c/o 127 Monks Dale
Yeovil
Somerset   BA21 3JE
Tel/fax: 01935 471641

Council for Education in World
Citizenship
15 St Swithin's Lane
London EC4N 8AL
Tel: 0171 929 5090

Appendix 2

Bibliography

Action on Aftercare Consortium (1996) *Too Much Too Young: the Failure of Social Policy in Meeting the Needs of Care Leavers*, Barnardo's.

Allan, Graham (1989) *Friendship, Developing a Sociological Perspective*, Harvester Wheatsheaf.

Aluffi-Pentini, Anna and Lorenze, Walter (eds.) (1997) *Anti-Racist Work with Young People, European Experiences and Approaches*, Russell House Publishing.

BBC (1989) *Crosby on Quality*, Training notes, BBC Enterprises.

Berne, E. (1979) *The Games People Play, The Psychology of Human Relationships*, Penguin.

Blanchard K. and Spencer, Johnson (1984) *The One Minute Manager*, Fontana.

Brannan (1994) *Young People, Health and Family Life*, Open University.

Bremner, Jeni, and Hilin, Anthony (1993) *Sexuality, Young People & Care*, CCETSW, (1994) Russell House Publishing.

Buchanan, Ann and Ten Brike, JoAnn, *What Happened When they were Grown up?*, University of Oxford.

Buchanan, Ann; Wheal, Ann; Walder, Daphne; Macdonald, Sue; and Coker, Ray (1993) *Answering Back*, University of Southampton.

Buchanan, Ann; Wheal, Ann and Barlow, Jane (1995) *How to Stay out of Trouble*, University of Oxford.

Buzan, T. with Buzan, B. (1993) *The Mind Map Book: Radiant Thinking*, BCA.

Canter, Lee (1992) *How to Help Improve Your Child's Behavior in School*, Lee Canter & Associates, USA.

Caring for Children (1997) paper on *Care and Control*, 3rd Draft.

Caring for Children (1997) paper on *Rights and Responsibilities*, 2nd Draft.

Caring for Children (1997) paper on *Early Intervention*, 1st Draft.

Chalk, Steve (1991) *Understanding Teenagers*, Kingsbury.

The Children Act 1989, HMSO.

Children's Legal Centre (1997) *At What Age Can I?*, The Children's Legal Centre.

Children's Society (1995) *Children in Focus*, The Children's Society.

Dacre, Dunlop (1996) *The Case for Sport*, Criminal Justice Matters.

Dover-Counsell, Jenny (1997) *Educational Therapy*, Young Minds Magazine.

Eldridge, Hillary and Still, Jenny, (1991) Course Notes, Various, Gracewell Institute.

Elkin, David (1994) *Ties That Stress, The New Family Imbalance*, Harvard University Press.

FICE (1997) *A Code of Ethics for People Working with Children and Young People*, FICE (Fédération Internationale des Communicatives Éducatives – Europe).

Freeman, Norman H. (1980) *Strategies of Representation in Young Children*, Academic Press.

Garratt, et al. (1997) *Changing Experiences of Youth*, Open University.

Geach, Peter T. (1976) *Reason and Argument*, Blackwell.

Guardian, The (1997) Various articles and reports, The Guardian Media Group.

Halsbury's Law of England, 4th Edition, vol.15, Butterworth Law Publishers Ltd.

Hampshire County Council (1995) *Positive Behaviour Management*, Tutor and Course notes, Hampshire County Council.

Hampshire Educational Psychology Service (1994) *Assertive Discipline*, Hampshire County Council.

Harris, Thomas A. (1979) *I'm OK – You're OK*, Pan.

Hevey, Denise (1990) *Workbook 2 Growth Points*, Open University.

Hooper, Rob (1997) *Counselling in Independent Schools,* Young Minds Magazine.

Hudson, John (1995) *Family Support,* John R Hudson Consultancies.

Internet @ccess Made Easy, October 1997, Paragon Publishing.

Kataz, Neil H. and Lawyer, John W. (1993) *Conflict Resolution, Building Bridges,* Sage Publications.

Kurtz, Zarrina (1994) *How can Social Services Help the Health Needs of Adolescents?*

McGuire, Christine (1997) *Health Promotion and the Family,* Highlight Barnado's/NCB.

Leadbetter, David and Trewarth, Robin (1996) *Handling Aggression and Violence at Work,* Russell House Publishing.

Luton, Kathleen; Booth, Graham; Leadbetter, Jane; Tee, Gillian and Wallace, Fiona (1991) *Positive Strategies for Behaviour Management,* NFER Nelson.

McPherson, Ann; Macfarlane, Aidan and Donovan, Chris (1996) *Health of Adolescents in Primary Care,* Royal College of General Practitioners.

Narramore, Bruce and Lewis, Vern C. (1990) *Parenting Teens: A Road Map through the Ages and Stages of Adolescence,* Tyndale.

Open University (1997) *Law Cards (Scotland)* and *Law Cards (Northern Ireland),* The Open University.

Parenting Forum Newsletter, no. 2 (1996) National Children's Bureau.

Parker, Roy; Ward, Harriett; Jackson, Sonia; Aldgate, Jane and Wedge, Peter (1992) *Looking after Children: Assessing Outcomes in Child Care,* HMSO.

Rees, Gwyneth (1997) *Hidden Truths, Young Peoples Experience of Running Away,* Childrens Society.

Roche, J. and Tucker (eds.) (1997) *Youth in Society: Contemporary Theory, Policy and Practice,* Open University.

Rogers, Wendy and Stainton Tucker, Stanley (1997) *Topic 1 Getting Started,* Open University.

Sandford, Amanda (1997) *Children and Smoking,* Highlight National Children's Bureau.

Sandole, Dennis J. D. and Merwe, Hugo van der (eds.) (1993) *Conflict Resolution Theory and Practice, Integration and Application*, Manchester University Press.

Saunders, Lesley and Broad, Bob (1997) *The Health Needs of Young People Leaving Care*, De Montfort University.

Schools Council U.K. *Aims and Objectives of a Schools Council*, Schools Council.

Segal, Judith W.; Chipman, Susan F. and Glaser, Robert (1985) *Thinking and Learning Skills, Vol 1*, Lawrence Erlbaum Associates, London.

Social Policy Research no. 106 (1996) *Parenting in the 1990s*, Joseph Rowntree Foundation.

Southampton University (1997) Bulletin, *Symptoms of Meningitis*, University of Southampton.

Statutory Instrument (1991) *Children and Young Persons (Secure Accommodation) Regulations 1991* and amendment 1992, HMSO.

Sutton, Carole, *Managing Difficult Children*, Books 1-6, HCSF.

Thomson, Rachael (ed.) Sex Education Forum (1993) *Religion, Ethnicity, Sex Education*, National Children's Bureau.

Thompson, Neil; Murphy, Michael and Stradling, Steve (1997) *Tackling Stress*, Child Care Forum.

Thompson, Neil; Murphy, Michael and Stradling, Steve with O'Neill, Paul (1996) *Meeting the Stress Challenge*, Russell House Publishing.

Tucker, Stanley (1997) K201 *Working With Young People, Introduction Study Guide*, The Open University.

Waldman, Julia and Waldman, Keith (1996) *Whose Sport?*, Criminal Justice Matters.

Wells, Rosemary (1997) *Helping Children Cope with Divorce*, Sheldon Press.

West Yorkshire Youth Fax Consortium (1995) *A Rough Guide for Living*, Yorkshire Radical.

Wheal, Ann (1995) *The Foster Carer's Handbook*, Russell House Publishing.

Wheal, Ann in collaboration with Buchanan, Ann (1994) *Answers: A Handbook for Residential and Foster Carers of Young People 11-18 years,* Longman.

Wheal, Ann and Waldman, Julia (1997) *Friends and Family as Carers,* National Foster Care Association.

World Health Organisation (1920) *W.H.O. Constitution,* W.H.O. New York.